Praise for

Simple Money, Rich Life

"Bob Lotich walks the talk. In *Simple Money, Rich Life,* he's giving away all the tips, tricks, and tactics he's employed to personally overcome $400,000 in debt and hit his own generosity stretch goal of giving away $1 million. His story is amazing, but it doesn't have to be unique! This book is full of big steps made in faith, and it's also full of practical actionable advice to help you reach your own financial goals."

—MARK BATTERSON,
New York Times bestselling author of *Win the Day*

"Bob is uniquely gifted to take a topic (money) that most tend to find overwhelming and actually make it simple. If that isn't unique enough, he (with Linda's help) delivers the lessons with grace in a non-judgmental tone that leaves you gently challenged, excited, and inspired with your finances."

—CARLOS WHITTAKER, author of *Enter Wild*

"Some books are exceptionally helpful; others can totally change your life. *Simple Money, Rich Life* is the latter. Bob Lotich will guide you through each step on the path of reaching true financial freedom. Buy it. Read it. Apply it."

—CHUCK BENTLEY, CEO of Crown Financial Ministries

"Are you frustrated that it feels like you are always behind financially and every time you make some bit of progress, there's another emergency that sets you back again? *Simple Money, Rich Life* will inspire and encourage you that there is hope—even if you have an empty bank account, looming bills, piles of debt, and a too-small paycheck. Best of all, this book will teach you how to not just survive but thrive, and to ultimately be in a position to generously give and make a difference in the lives of others!"

—CRYSTAL PAINE, *New York Times* bestselling author and founder of moneysavingmom.com

"I believe in discernment and discipline over deprivation, so I've never been into books that preach hyperfrugality. *Simple Money, Rich Life* is approachable yet packed with biblical inspiration, timeless wisdom, and fresh strategies and tactics that can help you create a truly rich life."

—PATRICE WASHINGTON, award-winning host of
the *Redefining Wealth* podcast

"Bob succeeds where other financial gurus fail: he tells you not only what to do but how precisely to do it. And he does it all in a way that is centered on Jesus and his gospel. Highly recommended!"

—JORDAN RAYNOR, bestselling author of *Redeeming Your Time*

"There is so much *gold* in this book! Effective money management can sometimes feel like a daunting prospect, but this book is the perfect balance between principles, practical strategies, and inspiration, with actionable steps you can start applying right away."

—RUTH SOUKUP, *New York Times* bestselling author of
Living Well Spending Less

"Bob and Linda see money and generosity through a completely different lens than most. I admire them greatly. Their authenticity, depth of wisdom, and heart to advance God's Kingdom are deeply inspiring. This book is your invitation and guidebook to a financial life that you never dreamed possible."

—JOSHUA BECKER, founder of Becoming Minimalist and author of
The Minimalist Home

"Within these pages lies the blueprint for you to move from merely surviving to thriving financially. The practical wisdom that you will learn will propel you to take action and experience the peace that comes with proper financial stewardship."

—TALAAT MCNEELY, CEO of His and Her Money

"I love this book. If you're bored with the plethora of teachings out there about money, saving, and giving, or think you've heard it all, Bob Lotich will surprise you. Fresh, unpredictable, practical, and even entrepreneurial, *Simple Money, Rich Life* is a book you'll be glad you read and applied."
—CAREY NIEUWHOF, bestselling author of *At Your Best*

"In *Simple Money, Rich Life,* Bob and Linda share exactly how to quickly take control of your money and reveal a fresh approach to stewardship. Their teaching style is easy to understand, won't leave you feeling guilty for past mistakes, and will inspire and strengthen your faith so you can truly live a rich life."
—ALEX SEELEY, author of *The Opposite Life*

"Money is hard. Making it, managing it, paying the bills, having enough to go around and not losing your mind in the process—it's really hard! Want to know how to make it easy? Find someone who's done that successfully, who's willing to teach you and then walk with you step-by-step. No judging, no guilt—just simple, easy-to-understand lessons that will fill your heart and soul with giddy joy. Bob Lotich's done all of that (and boy, does he have a story!) and boiled it down to a simple four-part plan. What you hold in your hands is a golden opportunity to make your money simple and your life rich."
—MARY HUNT, author of *Debt-Proof Living*

Simple Money, Rich Life

Simple Money,

Rich Life

ACHIEVE TRUE FINANCIAL FREEDOM
& DESIGN A LIFE OF ETERNAL IMPACT

BOB LOTICH

WATERBROOK

Published in the United States by WaterBrook, an imprint of Random House, a division of Penguin Random House LLC.

WATERBROOK® and its deer colophon are registered trademarks of Penguin Random House LLC.

Library of Congress Cataloging-in-Publication Data
Names: Lotich, Bob, author.
Title: Simple money, rich life : achieve true financial freedom and design a life of eternal impact / Bob Lotich.
Description: First edition. | Colorado Springs : WaterBrook, [2022] | Includes bibliographical references.
Identifiers: LCCN 2021050843 | ISBN 9780593193655 (trade paper) | ISBN 9780593193662 (ebook)
Subjects: LCSH: Wealth—Religious aspects—Christianity. | Finance, Personal—Religious aspects—Christianity. | Money—Biblical teaching. | Money—Religious aspects—Christianity.
Classification: LCC BR115.W4 L685 2022 | DDC 241/.68—dc23/eng/20211115
LC record available at https://lccn.loc.gov/2021050843

Printed in the United States of America on acid-free paper

waterbrookmultnomah.com

3rd Printing

SPECIAL SALES Most WaterBrook books are available at special quantity discounts when purchased in bulk by corporations, organizations, and special-interest groups. Custom imprinting or excerpting can also be done to fit special needs. For information, please email specialmarketscms@penguinrandomhouse.com.

CONTENTS

AUTHOR'S NOTE

If you're anything like me, when you start a new book you're probably a little curious about the author. And you might wonder what he looks like, if he has a weird accent, and, of course, whether he is a dog person or cat person.

For the past 15 years, I have been a full-time blogger, podcast host, and money coach at seedtime.com. Maybe our paths have crossed and you already know all this about me and more.

But if we haven't met yet, grab your phone and visit seedtime .com/hello for a short video from my wife, Linda, and me. We'd love the chance to give you a virtual high five as we set off on this journey together.

Either way, as you read, know that Linda and I have been praying for you. You aren't holding this book by accident. Whether you're currently on a financial mountaintop or in a valley, know that God has much more He wants to do in and through you.

So, go ahead and cozy up with (your favorite animal), grab a cup of (your favorite drink), and let's get to it.

Cheering you on,
Bob Lotich

INTRODUCTION

It was March 5, 2002, the day before my 21st birthday. I had just left the beach and was driving my convertible down a busy Florida road in front of a minor-league ballpark. I had just gotten paid, it was 75 degrees and sunny, and my two best friends were flying in to celebrate my birthday. From the outside looking in, I was living the dream, which made it easy to hide the truth of my financial situation.

Right then my car engine died in the middle of the road. It was so unexpected that I didn't even have time to pull it over to the shoulder. I flipped on my hazard lights, hoping to not get rear-ended as my car rolled to a stop. Panicking, I tried to start the car again and again and again. After about eight attempts, I gave up.

I had no one to call for help. Everyone I knew was at least 1,000 miles away. And my Nokia cell phone's greatest feature was the *Snake* game, not the Uber app.

I looked around and saw a guy directing cars into the ballpark. I walked over to ask if he could help me push the car out of the middle of the road. He said no. *That's okay,* I thought. *With hundreds of cars driving by, I'm sure someone will stop and help.* But no one did. *Cool.*

Trying to keep my male ego intact, I played it cool and acted like I had it all under control. *Don't mind me, I'll just be over here in the middle of this busy street awkwardly pushing my car while steering with one arm.*

Eventually I managed to get the car to the shoulder and climbed inside. I sat down and had my freak-out moment as despair began to creep in. I thought through the events that would likely unfold as I realized that my entire financial life was basically a house of cards on a windy day. The truth of my financial mess had finally become impossible to hide.

I'd been on my way to the bank to cash my paycheck so I could pay my rent that was due in about three hours. If I was late, the landlord would tack on a $50 fee. But my paycheck was just enough to cover the rent, so there was no way I could come up with that extra $50. I had no savings—only $7 in my checking account—and I'd been living off the $264 of available credit left on my credit card.

And now my car's worn-out alternator (a $60 part) was about to kick off a financial catastrophe. It's amazing how fast a great day can go south when you're living paycheck to paycheck.

Fighting back tears, I grabbed the steering wheel with the same intensity as the fear gripping my heart and mind. I was clueless about what to do next.

As cars continued to drive by, I desperately wanted just a little help, a hug, or someone to tell me it was going to be okay. I felt ashamed, embarrassed, and completely alone.

At this point I wasn't even thinking about how I was going to survive the following weeks or months. Or the fact that I was in a very fast downward spiral with my finances. All I could focus on was the current crisis I found myself in.

This wasn't how my life was supposed to turn out. I had grown up wanting to be an accountant (yes, weirdos like me exist). I had worked at a bank and thought I knew everything about money. So, why was I living paycheck to paycheck, broken down in the middle of the road, racking my brain to figure out how to tow and fix my car with only hours left before my rent was due?

The truth is, everything I had learned and believed about money came from the wrong sources. And because I hadn't even thought to invite God in, I had this mess to show for it.

I thought the answer to my money problems was simply that I

needed *more* money. But I didn't actually need more money (though you could have never convinced me of that then). I needed to learn how to better manage what I had been given.

Sitting in that broken-down convertible with my head in my hands, I cried out to God through hot tears and prayed for wisdom. I decided right then and there that whatever it took, I had to end this financial chaos.

If God had a different path, I was ready to follow.

OUR MONEY EDUCATION HAS COME FROM THE WRONG PLACES

I used to assume my financial mess was just my own bad luck. And sure, we all get dealt different hands. Some people have some big obstacles to overcome. But the truth is, I had been dealt a pretty decent middle-class hand, yet I was still a mess.

Why was that?

I have come to believe that it's because you and I have a lot working against us.

As much as I enjoyed learning how to write cursive and how the Dewey decimal system works, I would argue that knowing how to earn, save, and manage money is essential to almost every human—as important as any subject we learned in school. Yet most of us have received little to no financial education.

This lack of education creates a void that will inevitably be filled one way or another. And so our money "education" has come from all the wrong places. Most of our beliefs about money come from those who have no business teaching us about it: well-meaning (but broke) friends and family, celebrities, Instagram influencers, and credit card companies, to name a few. Even if they aren't explicitly teaching us about money, their influence has become the de facto financial education that far too many receive.

And for those of us who sought out a financial education by reading books, the fact is that bookstores are full of money books pushing the world's flawed approach. Many don't work, and those that do help you succeed at the wrong thing. It's no wonder we tend to believe that financial success is complicated or that true financial freedom isn't possible.

Like me, at the end of my rope in my broken-down convertible, many of us end up with stacks of overdue bills as we count down the days to payday. And an inability to build decent savings. And a week full of Mondays as we drag ourselves to unfulfilling jobs just because we have to pay the bills. And never-ending money fights with our spouses as we just try to survive.

And to top it all off, many of us feel guilt and shame for not managing money better, when it might not have been our fault in the first place.

The world's way of handling money has failed us. It's time for a new approach.

THE SIMPLE FORMULA

It began with John Wesley, a famed English evangelist and theologian. In one of his writings from the 18th century, I found this:

> I gain all I can (namely, by writing) without hurting either my soul or body. I save all I can, not willingly wasting any thing, not a sheet of paper, not a cup of water. . . . Yet by giving all I can, I am effectually secured from "laying up treasures upon earth." Yea, and I am secured from either desiring or endeavouring it, as long as I give all I can.[1]

Over the past 15 years, I've been guided by what the Bible says about money, as well as Wesley's words that have served as the primary inspiration for this four-part formula:

Earn all you can. Save all you can. Give all you can. Enjoy it all.

As Linda and I applied this biblically inspired formula to our finances, we began to see miracle after miracle. Our world quickly began changing:

- We were unified with our finances like we had never been before.

- I found work that I was called to, was fulfilling, and actually paid well.

- For the first time in our adult lives, we weren't stressed about money.

- Our savings accounts began to fill up, and we began investing for the future.

- We paid off all our debt by age 31—credit cards, car loans, student loans, and even our house.

- We found ourselves giving more than we dreamed possible. And it became one of our biggest passions in life.

Simply put, we began thriving financially. And it wasn't contingent on our income. Sometimes our income was up; sometimes it was down. Regardless of where life's roller coaster took us, we realized we could thrive.

What if the key to a thriving financial life was simpler than you ever thought possible?

TACTICS, STRATEGIES, AND PRINCIPLES

This formula isn't the *only* way to win with money, but it's by far the best approach I have found in my 15-plus years of study. While I will certainly share my favorite tactics and strategies, the bulk of this book consists of timeless principles—principles you can rely on year after year for the rest of your life, regardless of the financial hand you have been dealt.

There is one fundamental piece to all this, though: you need all four parts to work together. The power is in their synergy. Just one by itself is considerably weaker than when all four are working together.

As you and I do our part, God will show up and do His. And—no surprise—His part is the big part. Most of the book is designed to help us get in the position that will allow Him to do what He does best.

WHAT THIS BOOK IS NOT

Just so there isn't any confusion, let's get clear about what this book is *not*.

1. It Isn't About Manipulating God into Making You Rich

Following Jesus for how He can prosper us is kind of like marrying someone for money. It's a shell of a relationship. Jesus is the true prize, and God loves us too much to let us settle for anything less. And yes, like any good father, God loves to bless His kids, but chasing the provision rather than the Provider is a mistake. Jesus is always our greatest gift and treasure, far greater than any financial blessings that may come our way.

2. It Isn't a Theological Discourse About Money

This book isn't a theological dissertation; it's an operating manual. We are going to explore some biblical financial concepts, but I also want to arm you with practical advice and tools that are easy to understand and apply. My goal is to connect the dots between the most important financial concepts and the timeless principles laid out in the Bible and then translate them into a highly actionable plan.

3. It Isn't a Guilt and Shame Party

Plenty of financial books try to use guilt to get us to take action. Not this one. I'm not a trust-fund baby who has never known what it's like to experience financial challenges. I've been there. The struggle is real. But the shame I felt about my money situation was only harming me. I didn't need any more added to the pile. So you won't find that in this book. Linda and I will gently stretch your beliefs about money and encourage you to trust in our unfailing God. Consider us good friends helping you become the best version of yourself.

4. It Isn't About *Not* Enjoying Anything in Life

Balance tends to be a struggle for many people when it comes to money. I've seen some people spend every last dime while living for the here and now and some who fearfully hoard every last dime for the future. It's easy to fall to the extremes and miss the mark. This book is going to address both sides so we can walk in a healthy balance to enjoy the moment, enjoy the future, and enjoy giving in light of our eternal purpose.

5. It Isn't a One-Size-Fits-All Approach

You might be doing well financially, or you might be broke. You might have an income as steady as the sun, or you might have never had a consistent income in your life. You might be recovering from uncontrollable spending, or you might be dealing with a crisis through no fault of your own. Because there is no one-size-fits-all approach to money, I promise you there will be something that does *not* fit your situation. That's inevitable when talking about money. But the principles we'll discuss are universal, so if a tactic doesn't apply then just focus on the principle behind it.

WHAT THIS BOOK IS

With that out of the way, let's talk about what this book is: a simple framework that will help you live a truly rich life and make a significant eternal impact. And while the principles contained in it will help you have more money, our definition of a rich life is much further reaching. It's a life of significance, of unparalleled peace, where you are enslaved to no one, free to obey however God leads, and able to enjoy the overflow of generosity in your life.

If you want to experience a truly rich life, this book will show you how, regardless of your current income level. It will require you to do away with old patterns of thinking and change a few old habits as well. But stick with me, and you're going to enjoy the ride.

HOW THE BOOK IS LAID OUT

Simple Money, Rich Life is laid out in four distinctly different parts. And while all four parts are designed to work together, feel free to jump around to your heart's content, or just read front to back.

Part 1: Save All You Can

This section will give you incredibly practical tips and suggestions to help you reframe how you spend money and free up hundreds of dollars a month. You will be a much smarter spender and will have strategies in place to better manage your money for the rest of your life. We're starting with the save section because it's important to have these foundational concepts down before you start earning more.

Part 2: Earn All You Can

Whether you're an employee, freelancer, stay-at-home parent, business owner, or anything else, this section will help you increase your earning potential. And not with get-rich-quick tactics that rarely work and never last. Instead, we'll examine the keys to earning more in the digital era that we find ourselves living in.

Part 3: Give All You Can

I designed this section to help you see giving in a whole new light. It starts not with giving more but with giving differently. It transforms giving from an obligation into the real adventure of a lifetime that God invites us to join Him on. It also provides practical strategies to help you grow in your generosity and make it more fun than you ever thought possible.

Part 4: Enjoy It All

We can save, earn, and give while being miserable, or we can enjoy it all. Linda and I have come to view it all as worship, as the blessing that it is. This section will focus on how we can enjoy each moment of our financial lives—even the difficult ones.

THE 21-DAY KICK-START

At the end of each of the four parts are five challenges to help you apply what you've learned. Then we have one very important challenge at the end to top it all off. Feel free to do one challenge each day or all five in one day. You get to choose your own adventure here. The challenges are designed to extract some of the most important concepts from the book and give you simple action steps to begin implementing them.

> ## Simple Insight
>
> Visit seedtime.com/bonus to sign up for daily reminders to stay on track with the challenges. You'll probably want to bookmark this page as well because it contains all of the helpful tools and resources shared in this book.

Now for the most important part. With most nonfiction books, the massive impact comes not from reading but from *acting* on what you have read. So don't just read the book. If you want to see changes, then take action. Sound good?*

LINDA IS GOING TO BE JOINING US

I like to tell people that I'm a high-performance money coach married to a high-performance spender. Like most married couples, we're on the same page about some aspects of our financial life—but not all. So my lovely wife, Linda, is going to be chiming in throughout the book like this:

> **LINDA:** Hello there, nice to meet you! If you can't already tell from that introduction, I'm the fun one! I'm here to make sure this doesn't read like any other money book you've ever picked up. If you're married, I might just be the voice of reason to your spouse. Or maybe to you. Either way, I'll be dropping in to encourage you, share a spouse's (and a spender's) perspective, and remind us all not to take this stuff too seriously.

---

* Giving you a virtual high five *Top Gun* style.

Bob & Linda

PHOTO © JOSIAH DAMERY

WE ARE ALL ON A JOURNEY

For more than 15 years, I have been studying every Bible verse about money and seeking out every practical strategy for mastering my money. Thanks to the internet and the mind-blowing grace of God, I've had the privilege of sharing money-management techniques, budgeting tips, and investing strategies with over 50 million Seed-Time readers, podcast listeners, and students. I also have the honor of being a financial coach and a Certified Educator in Personal Finance®, and I'm proud to call myself a money nerd.

And yet, even with all this "experience," I still occasionally do dumb things with money. Just like you, I'm on a journey. A journey of continually learning and getting better with money. And to better understand what God is saying to us through the Bible.

So, let's just imagine that you and I are having coffee. I'm not your financial advisor suggesting a change to your retirement plan. I'm not your pastor trying to counsel you. Just consider me a friend sharing the tips, tools, and revelations that God has used to do a complete 180 in our financial lives and the lives of those in our Seed-Time community.

Let's pray and invite God into this journey, expecting Him to show up.

Ready? Let's go.

PART 1

SAVE ALL YOU CAN

If you would be wealthy, think of saving,
as well as of getting.

—BENJAMIN FRANKLIN

I carried our newborn into our dimly lit bedroom at 3 a.m. and found Linda curled up on the floor, sobbing. As I helped her to her feet, she put her head on my shoulder and through tears said, "I can't do this anymore."

She had birthed our third child the week before and was in the new-baby sleep deprivation phase. We'd experienced this phase before, but this time was different.

A few weeks earlier, she had developed a rash. It began on her stomach and spread to her arms and legs. It was so itchy that she was able to sleep only a total of one or two hours a night. The only thing that brought even a hint of relief was a cold shower, and she was taking 10 to 15 a day, desperate to get a few minutes of relief.

I called doctors, spent hours on the internet researching, and bought every cream, pill, and concoction that Amazon and Walgreens sold. We had tried every suggestion from dermatologists, naturopaths, and even the top "experts" (aka Facebook), but nothing worked.

After many days of this, while we dealt with a newborn and two little kids, the sleep deprivation had gotten so bad that Linda was beginning to hallucinate. I wanted nothing more than to fix this problem and end my wife's suffering. Yet no matter how hard I tried, nothing seemed to work. Now here I was in the middle of the night, in our uncharacteristically disheveled bedroom, holding my dear wife and feeling utterly helpless.

We both hoped that it would just get better as the days went by. But as we entered the second week, we had the terrifying revelation that it was not going away and it was actually getting worse. It continued for another week and then another with no improvement.

After a month, Linda called her ob-gyn, who happened to also be a good friend and well aware of Linda's condition. That morning, as I wrestled with the baby and quieted the other kids, God intervened.

In the middle of the conversation, the ob-gyn remembered the details of an allergic reaction that Linda had had many years before to a particular medicine. She had been taking the medicine all throughout the pregnancy with no reaction at all, but according to our doctor friend, being pregnant can sometimes suppress certain allergic reactions. Now that Linda was no longer pregnant, she theorized that the reaction could be back.

We had tried so many things that others had suggested. We had gotten our hopes up so many times over those torturous weeks, only to be disappointed every time. We were both so worn down from trying stuff that Linda wasn't even sure it was worth testing. The likelihood was that nothing would come of it at all—just like the dozens of other attempts that had failed.

But I convinced Linda that it was worth pausing the medicine for a weeklong test to see what would happen. Within a day, the itchiness began to subside, and she was soon able to sleep like a normal mom of a newborn.

LINDA: Never could I have imagined that the normal amount of sleep with a newborn would be so refreshing!

We had tried everything and gotten nowhere. But that one divinely inspired memory was the key that unlocked the solution.

Sometimes you try thing after thing after thing with no success. Disappointment settles in, and it feels reasonable to assume that if all these things failed, then nothing will work. However, the truth is, you might have a key chain with 25 keys on it but only one is going to actually unlock the door for you.

It doesn't matter that you have tried 10, 15, or 20 times with no success. There is a key on that key chain that will open the door. And when you find the right one, it can change everything.

FINANCIALLY STUCK

Has your financial life ever felt like this? Maybe you have tried all the budgets, expert financial advice, and debt-payoff plans but nothing has worked. Maybe you are so worn down from trying stuff that you have all but given up. Maybe you are flat-out convinced that if there were a better way, you would have discovered it by now.

I know that feeling of being stuck in a dark hole where despair sinks in and you can't imagine climbing out. I've been there. Then I found that one seemingly tiny change—that one key—that changed our world forever.

In this section, I'm going to share many simple, God-inspired ideas that have blown our minds. Just like Linda did after taking every pill, using every lotion, and trying every trick to get rid of that rash, we finally found the one thing that made all the difference.

THE FIRST PART OF THE FORMULA: SAVE ALL YOU CAN

Just to be clear, when I say "save all you can," it isn't just about filling up a savings account. Instead, the focus is on reducing expenses and saving money on things that you regularly purchase, which will in turn provide you with more available income.

Most people tend to think that their money problems are a result of not having enough income. And for some of us, that is the case, but I have found that the vast majority of people in the Western world can feel a lot wealthier without earning any more money. It's all about finding hidden money in the most unexpected places.

You're probably thinking one of two things right now:

1. *Where is all this money going to come from? I'm already careful and diligent, so there is no way hidden money is just sitting around.* (Hang tight. We'll get there.)

2. *Oh no. This must be one of those penny-pinching, hyperfrugality books.* (Don't worry. I am not that guy. This is not that book.)

I am more into big wins that don't have a huge effect on my standard of living. I don't want to live like a pauper, and the good news is, we don't have to. I live and breathe this stuff. I specialize in (and get a thrill from) finding the most painless methods that yield the biggest results. As a matter of fact, you'll probably find that this section alone will pay for this book many times over.

We're going to dig into a lot of new ideas, so keep an open mind and be willing to try new things. By the end of this first part, I believe you're going to be on your way to some big financial wins.

CHAPTER 1

THE BATTLE IS HIS,
BUT YOU HAVE TO SHOW UP

For the past few years, four simple words posted on my office wall have served as a constant reminder of God's role in the challenges I face:

The battle is His.

About 3,000 years ago, the people of Judah had three separate armies coming to wage war against them.* They were vastly outnumbered, and they recognized their weakness: "We have no power to face this vast army that is attacking us. We do not know what to do, but our eyes are on you."[1] Judah knew they couldn't win this battle alone. So they turned to God.

Then the prophet Jahaziel spoke up, saying, "Listen, King Jehoshaphat and all who live in Judah and Jerusalem! This is what the LORD says to you: 'Do not be afraid or discouraged because of this vast army. For the battle is not yours, but God's.'"

He continued, "Tomorrow march down against them. . . . You will not have to fight this battle. Take up your positions; stand firm and see the deliverance the LORD will give you, Judah and Jerusalem. Do not be afraid; do not be discouraged. Go out to face them tomorrow, and the LORD will be with you."[2]

---

* This is one of my favorite stories in the Bible. Go look up 2 Chronicles 20, and notice how God not only solved their problem but also provided a huge blessing that they would have missed if they hadn't shown up.

Did you catch that? God required the army of Judah to march down to the battle line. If God was going to fight the battle for them, then why couldn't they just sit inside the walls of the city, where it was comfortable and safe?

Yes, the battle was the Lord's, but they had to show up. The same is true of your financial situation—the battle is the Lord's, but *you* have to show up.

LET HIM FIGHT YOUR FINANCIAL BATTLE

I know firsthand how discouraging it is when you're looking at massive debt, insufficient income, or never-ending expenses and feel like you'll never be able to overcome it.

I remember looking at my mountain of debt and thinking, *I'm never going to get this paid off.* Then I compared that with our tiny salaries, and it honestly felt hopeless. I mean, it seemed like there was only about $50 left at the end of the month. It seriously looked like it would take 30 years to become debt-free.

But here is the thing. Our God is in the business of freeing people from bondage. I know that includes the bondage of sin, but I'm convinced it also includes financial bondage—especially debt.

Let me share a secret with you. You want to know what testimony I have heard more than anything else from our SeedTime community? It goes something like this:

We had [a huge amount of debt] that we wanted to pay off. When we looked at our income, it looked like it would take us [a crazy amount of time] to get it paid off. We felt discouraged and wondered whether our effort would even make a difference. But we prayed and felt God leading us to do [an unconventional thing that we thought wouldn't help at all]. But we decided to obey His leading. As we did, we saw the debt paid off way faster than we ever dreamed possible. We have no doubt this was God's doing.

This is our story too. As we took steps and trusted God to do His part, we experienced miracles and watched our mountain of debt disappear within about three years.

No matter how big your financial challenge is, the battle isn't yours. The battle is the Lord's. But *you* have to show up. Don't make the mistake of thinking that because it's His battle, He won't require you to do *something*. And often that something has to be done before you see the miracle:

- Jehoshaphat and Judah had to march down to the battle line against a far superior army *before* God delivered them.

- Moses had to walk up to the Red Sea and stretch out his staff *before* it parted.

- The disciples had to begin distributing the food *before* it was multiplied to feed the 5,000.

If they hadn't acted on their faith, do you think those miracles would have happened?

God is bigger than any financial problem we face, but we have to be willing to step out in faith to see the miracle. Oftentimes that step of faith is a natural step that allows God to do the supernatural.

HOW TO OUTRUN A CHARIOT

I once heard Pastor Chris Durso preach a sermon with some insightful commentary on an easily overlooked verse. In 1 Kings, we see Elijah do something pretty crazy. "The LORD gave special strength to Elijah. He tucked his cloak into his belt and ran ahead of Ahab's chariot all the way to the entrance of Jezreel."[3]

Elijah outran a chariot, but before he did, he tied up his cloak. If God had given him supernatural speed but he'd been tripping on his cloak the whole way, he probably wouldn't have outrun the chariot.

Elijah took the *natural* step so the *supernatural* thing that God was going to do wouldn't be hindered.

> When we take the natural step while prayerfully asking God to do the supernatural, we open the door for the miraculous.

God wants to do the supernatural in your financial life, but what steps are you taking to allow the supernatural to flow unhindered? King Jehoshaphat and his army had to march to the battle line in order to see the miracle.* When we take the natural step while prayerfully asking God to do the supernatural, we open the door for the miraculous.

Could it be that some of the practical steps laid out in this book are going to allow God to do the supernatural in your life?

LINDA: I have found the biggest breakthroughs when I remember that my job is to take natural steps, which usually gets me out of God's way so He has room to do the supernatural. When we do our part, we see how big the mountain is, how impossible it is to scale without His help, which makes it clear who really deserves all the glory. And it becomes easy to point back to God, because when you see a miracle, you can't help but tell people! So, show up, do your part, and watch the deliverance of the Lord.

In the rest of the book, I'll lay out some simple steps that have made room for God to do the supernatural in our lives. The first is determining your AUM.

---

* Interesting sidenote: their answer to prayer came as soon as they began worshipping.

CHAPTER 2

AUM: THE SECOND MOST IMPORTANT METRIC*

f you've ever started a weight-loss program, you know the first step is hopping on the scale. Why? Because you want to see your starting point to be able to measure progress, right?

And if you're like most people, you continue to step on the scale weekly or maybe even daily. Why? Because you want to see whether you're making progress, right? You want to see whether all this work you're putting in is yielding any result.

For some reason, we tend to understand the importance of tracking and reporting with weight-loss goals but not with financial goals. You would never set a goal to lose 20 pounds and then measure success by how loose your sweatpants are. Sure, it may be an indicator that you're going in the right direction, but it's a terrible way to track progress.

When it comes to money, most people use the wrong metrics to track their financial progress and wonder why they aren't reaching their goals. If you're going by how things feel, you'll never see the full picture. You're seeing only part of the picture if you're looking at any of the following:

- how tight money feels at the end of the month

---

* No, you didn't zone out for the most important metric. I'm just saving it for part 3 to keep you in suspense.

- your checking account balance
- your credit card balance

Each is a metric that gives an incomplete picture of financial progress. Luckily, there is a much better way. For weight loss, it's a scale. For financial progress, it's what I call Assets Under Management (AUM).

Simple INSiGHT

Most assume that having a good income means you're doing well financially, but oftentimes that isn't true. On the other hand, some people assume that their low salary means they're doomed financially. And that definitely isn't true.

AUM is one number that conclusively tells you how you're doing financially. It shows you what is really going on with your money, instead of what you think (or hope) is going on. Many financial experts refer to this as your net worth, but I prefer AUM for two key reasons:

1. **It helps me keep a proper perspective of money and possessions.** Specifically that they aren't actually mine. Rather, I'm a manager (or steward) of what God has entrusted to me for a short time. When we understand that everything in our possession (houses, cars, money, etc.) is not actually ours but should be managed for His purposes and glory, AUM seems like a more accurate and appropriate name.

2. **The thought of any number being labeled my "net worth" is pretty insulting.** You and I are intricately and lovingly de-

signed by God for a unique purpose. We have so much value (regardless of our financial successes or failures) that Jesus came to die for us. To say that the sum of my worth is a particular dollar amount doesn't sit well with me. Additionally, when you believe that any amount of money defines your worth, you're more tempted to look to that number for your identity, rather than to God.

LINDA: Just to further Bob's point, I want to remind you that God knew you before the foundation of the world. He was extremely intentional about when you would be born. Only you can add to the world what God created you to add. You're so important and significant. Pushing through the difficult things—like money—will only increase your impact. In other words, you were born for this.

WHY AUM TRUMPS DEBT TRACKING

Some people use the amount of debt they have as their sole metric of financial success. The less debt, the better their progress. No debt? You win!

While debt elimination is a great goal, using it as a tracking tool doesn't give you the full picture of what is going on in your financial life. AUM will allow you to continue tracking your financial progress even if you've eliminated all your debt. And trust me—there is a financial life *after* you pay off debt.

LINDA: Yeah, baby! And it's so good!

And if that wasn't enough, AUM is just more encouraging. When you track your progress by looking at your debt, you're seeing only the fruit of paying down those debts. On the other hand, your AUM can increase with every good financial decision you make.

For example, you can increase your AUM with the following actions:

- paying off credit cards or car loans

- paying more toward your mortgage

- buying property

- funding a Roth IRA

- contributing to your 401(k) or 403(b)

- adding money to savings

- buying index funds, mutual funds, or dividend-paying stocks

- even just not spending as much money

By using AUM as your metric to track, you'll find there are far more opportunities to move the financial needle than just paying off debts. So if you want to see constant progress toward your money goals, then start tracking your AUM, my friend.

CALCULATE YOUR AUM

Determining your AUM is really just a second-grade math problem. Take your assets (things you own), and subtract your debts. Here's the breakdown.

Total Your Assets

First, list every asset you can think of. Your house, vehicles, retirement accounts, investments, savings accounts, checking accounts, emergency fund, jewelry, and anything else similar would fall in this category. Really anything that has a dollar value or that you could realistically sell.

To get real estate values, you can use zillow.com to get a rough estimate of what your home is worth. For automobiles, check out KBB.com to see what they could be sold for. For all your checking, savings, and investment accounts, check the balances online or use your most recent statement.

You can include any items around your house that have value, but I suggest being conservative. For the purposes of sanity and simplicity, I don't bother with items under about $250. Yeah, I'm sure I could find someone on eBay to buy my socks, but I'm just looking for a general picture. I lump all these smaller items together on one line called "Misc. Items" and take a conservative guess as to what they could be sold for.

Once you have everything listed with the estimated value, total your assets.

Your Kick-START

Want to jump ahead and complete your related challenge?

Go to page 88 for details.

Total Your Debts (Liabilities)

A few lines below the asset total, you're going to list every debt you have. Mortgages, car loans, credit cards, student loans, medical debt, that money you borrowed from Grandma—they all apply. Do the same as above, checking balances on each one, and then total your debts.

Subtract Them

Now you can subtract your debt total from your asset total, and—voilà!—you have your AUM. Date it and save it.

Where to Do This

If you're into paper, do it on paper. Or you can calculate it using a simple worksheet like this:[*]

Assets	
Car	$10,000
House	$195,000
Savings	$5,000
401(k)	$10,000
Total Assets:	**$220,000**

Debts	
Car Loan	$5,000
Mortgage	$160,000
Student Loan	$10,000
Credit Card	$5,000
Total Debts:	**$180,000**

Assets Under Mgmt:	**$40,000**

OUR STARTING POINT

When Linda and I first calculated our AUM, it was -$13,843.84. I knew we had a bunch of debt, but I didn't realize we would be in the negative.

Initially I was discouraged. It felt like I was at the bottom of a hole, looking up, unsure where to go. But I noticed that as we began doing *slightly* less dumb things with our money, each month our AUM was increasing. After one year, it was up nearly $15,000 to $746! We were pretty thrilled just to no longer have a negative AUM—even if it was

[*] Grab your free copy here: seedtime.com/aum.

less than $800. And as we kept working on it, it just continued to grow.

Simple Insight

It's actually pretty common to start out with a negative AUM. Some people find they are in the red by six figures (often because of student loans or medical debt). Remember, it's not about where you are right now. It's about acknowledging the truth of your situation. No matter your initial AUM, call it what it is: a starting point for your financial testimony.

I normally check our AUM one or two times a year. But if you're working hard at it and need the encouragement, check it more! Regardless of what your number is, just look at it as the beginning. If you're increasing your assets by making good buying decisions or minimizing debts, your AUM will likely be growing.

GOD AND YOUR AUM

AUM is simply a tool to measure the progress of God's assets under our management. And good managers pay attention to what they are responsible for, right?

We aren't tracking it to impress others, to feel good about ourselves, or to determine our worth.

LINDA: Remember, Jesus showed all of us our worth by coming to earth, living a sinless life, and dying on the cross. No dollar amount can compare to the price He paid, because there is simply no number great enough to show what you are worth.

When we truly grasp that, we can see AUM as a tool to

measure progress and show His faithfulness and never as a number that describes significance.

Here's the thing: I believe God wants us to know exactly where we are financially so we can see and tell of His glory when He does the miraculous in our finances.

Moses was on the edge of the Red Sea *before* God parted it. I'm guessing He wanted the Israelites to get an up-close-and-personal view of the insurmountable obstacle in their path so they could better understand the magnitude of God's miracle in their lives. They would tell the story of His faithfulness for generations to come.

Regardless of your situation, find your starting point by calculating your AUM. In the years to come, it will be a reminder of how far God has brought you. And all the miraculous things that He does in your financial life will make your story that much richer.

CHAPTER 3

THE NEVER 100 RULE

Do you remember Mike Tyson? Heavyweight champion of the world. Fought Evander Holyfield and bit off part of his ear. How could we forget?

In 1997, during that infamous fight, he was disqualified after only three rounds and was paid $30 million. $30 million![1] For less than 10 minutes of fighting! And that was just for that one fight. Over the course of his career, he earned over $400 million.[2]

Now, Tyson may have had some other issues to deal with, but money wasn't one of them. He was set. Until 2003 . . . when he filed for bankruptcy, having spent it all (and an additional $23 million).

How could someone spend $423 million in a lifetime, let alone in just a few short years? This is so far beyond anything most people can understand that we tend to just dismiss it as an anomaly. But it isn't. Let's look at another scenario.

NBA players earn an average of $7.5 million a year.[3] And the average NFL player earns about $2.7 million a year.[4] Tyson's fortune aside, can you imagine what you could do with a measly $2.7 million salary?

LINDA: I'm sure I could figure something out.

Here's what's fascinating. Did you know that the majority of NBA and NFL players are broke shortly after they retire? According to

CNBC, "An estimated 60 percent of former NBA players go broke within five years of departing the league . . . [and] a reported 78 percent of former NFL players have gone bankrupt or [are] under financial stress just two years after retirement."[5]

> **LINDA:** That sure brings new meaning to those Kanye lyrics "win the Super Bowl and drive off in a Hyundai."[6]

I couldn't believe it when I read it. Even with millions of dollars at their disposal, many of our sports heroes are a financial mess. Yet most of us go to bed each night believing that if we just had a little more money, we would be able to get ahead financially.

> ## It's less about what's coming in. It's more about what you do with it.

We all want to believe the answer to our money problems is simply more money. But the truth is, it's less about what's coming in. It's more about what you do with it.[*]

THE NEVER 100 RULE EXPLAINED

You don't need to be a genius to guess that many pro athletes are making the same financial mistake that half of all Americans make.[7] They are spending 100% (or more) of their income each month. As a result, when that million-dollar salary is gone, they have nothing to show for it.

Now, maybe you already know all this. But in case you tend toward making some of the mistakes I have (you know, like spending my raise before it even showed up on my paycheck), I want to share

---

[*]   In fact, when you don't have the Never 100 Rule down, more money just amplifies the problem. This is why Mike Tyson found himself $23 million in the hole.

one rule that I like to follow that will ensure you have something to show, no matter your income.

I call it the Never 100 Rule. Simply put, *never spend 100% of your monthly income.*

It doesn't matter how wildly my income fluctuates; I do absolutely everything in my power to never spend 100% of what I earn that month.

By following this rule, you're giving yourself the best chance of financial success. And at the same time, you're greatly increasing your chances of avoiding the financial struggles of most Americans, including pro athletes.

On the other hand, if you consistently violate this rule, then you can be sure that you'll end up broke—no matter how much you earn. Ask Mike Tyson if you need proof.

Don't let the simplicity of this rule fool you. It will work if you have a huge income, if you have a small income, if you have been smart with money all your life, or if you are a financial mess (like Linda and I used to be). There isn't much one-size-fits-all financial advice, but this is about as close as it gets.

We could go through all the details of how to save more money each month, how to increase your income, or how to invest, but those details really don't matter much if you're spending 105% of your monthly income. If you want to succeed financially, you have to start with the Never 100 Rule.

MEET RONALD READ

Ronald Read was a gas-station attendant and janitor from Vermont. He never had a large income, but he consistently followed the Never 100 Rule. Over his 92 years of life, he avoided the financial stress experienced by so many pro athletes who earned 10 to 100 times more than him. That right there is pretty amazing if you think about it. But it gets better.

On a janitor's salary, he followed this rule and never spent his full paycheck. Instead, he consistently saved and invested. Over the course of his life, he amassed $8 million, most of which he chose to give away.[8]

Most of us believe that if we had an NFL salary for a few years, all our financial problems would be gone. Of course we wouldn't spend it all; we would do it differently. We would be so smart and wouldn't end up like 78% of retired NFL players. Right?

I hate to break it to you, but unless we're doing a good job managing what we have now, we won't manage more any better. It doesn't matter whether it is a 1,000% increase or just a 2% pay raise. Until we're prepared to handle the increase, no matter how big or small, it will be of little benefit to us.

WHEN IN CRISIS MODE

The truth is that a lot of us in the Western world are spending over 100% of our income each month because we're in crisis mode. From job loss to overwhelming medical bills to childcare expenses, it can seem like there is no way out. We borrow more and more, hoping that someday things will just fix themselves.

It's no wonder so many of us feel like we can't even think about saving and giving because we're so overwhelmed just trying to survive.

> LINDA: That feeling. That "this is never going to get better" feeling. I know it. I know the hopelessness. If you feel like that, know that we are praying for you and that there is a way out. That's what this book is for. Pray and open your mind as much as you can, and keep reading. Relief is on the way.

While Linda and I have walked through some tough financial battles, your situation will be different from ours or anyone else's. If you have given up hope and view it as impossible, then let me remind you that impossible situations are where God does His best work.

Living a truly rich life will require both natural steps and God's supernatural power. I've found that most people lean toward one or the other. They will either use wisdom with finances and expect that to be enough or choose to pray but ignore sound financial advice.

But I am telling you something amazing happens when both are working together—following the timeless financial wisdom laid out in the Bible and prayerfully stepping out in faith, giving God an opportunity to do a miracle.

So let's pray and invite God into your situation *and* use financial wisdom by starting with the Never 100 Rule. Choose to not spend 100% of your monthly income, and turn your attention to saving, investing, and giving in faith (more on this in later chapters). When we prayerfully and boldly attempt to do things God's way, He shows up.

THE NEVER 100 RULE IN ACTION

You're probably thinking, *This all sounds great on paper, but how do I do this in real life?* There is a four-part plan that will ensure you follow the Never 100 Rule and reach your financial goals. I call it the Straight-A Strategy, and it transformed our financial lives. Apart from God, this simple strategy deserves the most credit for helping us pay off our mortgage *in three years.**

As with anything else, some work will be involved. Simple doesn't mean magic. But it is so worth it. The Straight-A Strategy puts into practice four steps that we will break down in the next four chapters:

1. Attention

2. Automate

3. Adjust

4. Accountability

---

* Yes, you read that right. More on how we did this in a later chapter.

Regardless of whether your income follows the curve of a pro athlete, a career janitor, or anything in between, the Straight-A Strategy will give you the best chance of long-term success. It will ensure that your money goes where you want it to go and that you begin racing toward your financial goals faster than you thought possible.

CHAPTER 6

ATTENTION: WHEN PERFORMANCE
IS MEASURED, IT IMPROVES

Did you know that livestock was one of the earliest forms of currency?[1] Cows, sheep, goats, chickens, and other animals were the money of the day. So, even before people used precious metals to buy things, they used chickens and goats.

We see this as early as Genesis 13:2: "Abram had become very wealthy in livestock and in silver and gold." Did you catch that? Abram's wealth was first measured by *his livestock,* not his silver and gold.

Knowing that gives clarity to verses that we thought were only for shepherds and farmers—verses like Proverbs 27:23: "Know well the condition of your flocks, and pay attention to your herds."[2] This isn't just sage advice for farmers. It's instruction about handling money.

If livestock was a form of currency and farmers were instructed to know what was going on with their flocks, then wouldn't you think that would mean knowing how many goats, sheep, or cattle there were? It would mean knowing whether or not there was a wolf picking off a sheep each night, right?

Yet when it comes to our money, so many of us are like a farmer who just looks out the window into the field and says, "It looks like there are still some sheep out there. Not sure how many or if they are healthy or if a wolf is eating them, but it looks like there are some out there."

In *The Message* version of verses 23–24, we get even more clarity:

"Know your sheep by name; carefully attend to your flocks; (Don't take them for granted; possessions don't last forever, you know.)"

Not only are we instructed to know what's happening with our finances, but Proverbs also warns that we may not always have as much money as we do now. Just because you can pay all the bills and buy what you want doesn't mean that you will always be able to do so.

HERE IS A SEEDLING: YOU HAVE ONLY ONE JOB

Imagine that I gave you a seedling and one simple job. Your *only* job is to keep the seedling alive. You and pretty much any five-year-old would understand that in order to succeed at this task, you basically need to do two things:

- *not* put it in a closet

- pay attention to know when it needs water

As a backyard gardener, I have killed many plants in my day. And nearly every one of those casualties was a result of not paying attention to the plant. When I tell people that I like gardening, I often hear this response: "Oh, I just don't have a green thumb; I kill everything I plant." But if keeping a seedling alive is so simple, why do so many people have brown thumbs?

Nine times out of 10, they weren't paying attention to the plant and forgot to water it. And now they have developed a belief that they aren't good with plants simply because they weren't paying attention. The truth is, many people do exactly the same thing with money.

They weren't paying attention to their money, things didn't go how they hoped, and then they began saying they aren't good with money. However, they just need to attend to their flocks.

Know anyone like this?

This is such an underestimated key to financial success. Financial success, regardless of how you define it, requires that we pay attention and know what is going on. So, if you aren't already, let's start the habit today. The seedling starts small, but it will grow quickly.

Your future self (who looks really good, by the way) will look at your finances and be floored at how much progress you made. You'll break out of that paycheck-to-paycheck cycle, have more than enough, and be able to give way beyond your current level.

WHEN STORMS COME

In life, even if you do everything right with your seedling, storms still come. Jesus said this Himself.[3] So, how does a master gardener handle his plants when storms come?

By giving them *more* attention, not less. He continues to water the plants, but he also might prune broken branches or give them support.

When it comes to financial storms, the answer is not to ignore your finances but instead to focus more time and energy on them. When you lose your job or your transmission goes out, you don't ignore your budget. You focus more on it until the threat is gone.

LINDA: Raise your hand if you're like me and just want to ignore your problems and pretend everything will work out; well, you're not alone. But let's make a pact to do the hard things so we can become who God created us to be and fulfill His call on our lives!

A master gardener doesn't abandon his trees when they are struggling. Instead, he gives them extra time and attention until they are healthy again. Mastering our money requires the same of us. When a financial storm comes, we don't bury our heads in the sand but instead prayerfully do everything in our strength to weather it well.

CAREFULLY ATTEND TO YOUR MONEY

Karl Pearson, a 19th-century mathematician, has been credited with first articulating what is now known as Pearson's Law: "When performance is measured, performance improves. When performance is measured and reported back, the rate of improvement accelerates."[4]

Let's break down this law, starting with the first sentence: "When performance is measured, performance improves."

I've been driving a car nearly every day for more than 24 years. I can say with confidence that every time I've seen a cop on the side of the highway I've immediately slowed down. I might check my speed to determine how much I should slow down, but I always slow down. It doesn't matter whether I know my speed or not. The fact that I know my performance is being measured by the police officer causes me to improve.

> **LINDA:** Have you ever hidden the FedEx packages before your spouse saw them? Mmmm-hmmm, I see you! It's because you didn't want to have your "performance" measured by your spouse, right?
>
> Yeah, I have too. I used to try to "hide" a Starbucks addiction from Bob. Acting like he wouldn't see it on our bank statement. (You can't see me, but I'm rolling my eyes at myself.)
>
> One day, Bob saw the evidence. When I tried to nonchalantly throw it in the trash, he smiled and said, "Do you know you're spending about $200 on Starbucks each month? Do you know that adds up to about $2,400 a year?" My answer to all of that was "No." And though I pretended not to care, it got my attention.
>
> I thought about the things I wanted and why I could never seem to get them. It was because all that money was going to Starbucks. Once Bob told me the actual num-

bers, I couldn't help but think about what I could or should do to change.

To be clear, Bob never asked me to change or stop. He just presented the information with no judgment.

So, if you're hoping to talk with your spouse about his or her spending habits, then my advice is to just present facts with no tone of disapproval. Just allow him or her to have the information, and then—even if it's with gritted teeth—drop it.

SPEND LESS WITHOUT EVEN TRYING

Would you like to spend less money without even trying? We all would, right? Well, that's what this part of the Straight-A Strategy will do for you.

The first step is to pay attention to your spending. You could do this by writing down every purchase you make. This works really well. I've read stories of people cutting their spending by up to 50% (without even trying) simply by doing this exercise.

But I like keeping things as simple as possible. And since we're in the 21st century, there are some easier ways to get a lot of the benefit of this exercise, such as using an app like Personal Capital (my favorite at the time of publishing)[*] that will give you a detailed breakdown of your past spending within minutes.

Your Kick-Start

Want to jump ahead and complete your related challenge? Go to page 88 for details.

Here's what you do: First, you'll need to create a free account at

---

[*] Check seedtime.com/cashflow for my most up-to-date recommendation and a video walk-through of the process.

personalcapital.com. Then when you connect your spending accounts (credit card, checking account, etc.), Personal Capital will pull in a few months of past transactions. Under the Banking > Cash Flow > Expense tab,* you'll notice the app has attempted to categorize your purchases for you, but you'll want to review these for accuracy and adjust accordingly. Within just a few minutes, you'll be able to see exactly where you have spent your money for the past few months. For example, you'll have hard data showing whether you are anywhere close to the $500 you think you spend on groceries each month.

> **LINDA:** When we talk with students who have done this, they often end up finding hundreds of dollars of savings right off the bat! Blows my mind every time.

This is really exciting because this part of the Straight-A Strategy doesn't require us to attempt to make any actual changes to our spending. Just to measure and pay attention. And in doing so, things will automatically improve.

DON'T STOP THERE; TAKE IT UP A NOTCH

Let's amplify things a bit with the second half of Pearson's Law: "When performance is measured and reported back, the rate of improvement accelerates."

The key here is that getting regular updates on our performance helps us improve—and at a faster rate. So, looking back at our previous examples, we could speed up our progress by simply finding a way to track and report our performance. When I'm driving on the highway, I could use the Waze app, which can generate an audible alert when I drive five miles per hour over the speed limit. Or Linda

---

* At the time of printing, this is where you can find it.

could set up an SMS spending alert with the Mint app that would notify her when she spends $50 at Starbucks in a given month.

Remember, the pressure isn't on us to change our financial habits; we just need to track and get regular feedback. By doing so we perform better without even trying to change.

Lauren Cantoni, one of our students,* decided to take me up on this challenge to pay attention to her spending. Two months later, she said, "I cut my spending by over $800 each month. . . . and I feel more in control of my money than I ever have."

Before attempting to change our behavior, we should create systems that report our progress—kind of like a financial scoreboard.

THE MONEY GAME

In the book *The 4 Disciplines of Execution,* the authors share a post–Hurricane Katrina story that illustrates the critical importance of a scoreboard:

On the previous Friday night, the local high school team had played an important game. As expected, the stands were full, and there was the usual excitement leading up to the kickoff. But as the game progressed, something was missing. No one was cheering. In fact, no one seemed to be paying attention to the game at all. The only sound from the stands was the dull hum of conversation. What was happening?

The scoreboard had blown down during the hurricane and had not yet been repaired. The fans couldn't see any numbers. [Someone] described it this way: "No one could tell you what the score was, which down it was, or even how much time was left. There was a game going on, but it was like no one even knew."[5]

---

* She now helps coach our Real Money Method students to create a system for paying attention to and getting reporting on their spending.

Is this how you're treating your finances?

There is an incredibly important "game" going on and yet most people have no idea what's going on. And as a result, our

- financial stress increases

- marriages are struggling

- generosity suffers

- ability to follow God's call is hindered

And all this simply because we aren't paying attention to our finances? But what if we did?

Imagine the positive effects of tracking and reporting—even without trying to change your spending behavior. You could reduce financial stress, build a stronger marriage, grow in generosity, and know you're making an impact for the Kingdom. If we simply track and measure what's going on, then the financial progress we can make and the positive impact we can have are limitless.

CHAPTER 5

AUTOMATE: NEVER DEPEND ON WILLPOWER

I n 2008, I transitioned from working in a financial firm to running my own business. Do you know what surprised me the most? I had to pay taxes.

Sure, I had always known I was paying taxes, but I never really felt it. Taxes were nothing more than a line item on my paycheck. But now as a business owner, I was required (four times a year) to write an actual check to the IRS.

Paying taxes became very real. I watched my bank balance get chopped in half as I sent a huge portion of my hard-earned money to the IRS. Even though I paid much less (by amount and percentage of income) that first year than ever before, it hurt a lot more.

Why was this?

Previously, as an employee, paying taxes was automatic. I never thought about it because I never saw it. But as a business owner, I was forced to think about it. I was forced to see and feel the direct impact it had on my bank balance. And it was painful.

TAX COLLECTION IN THE US

During World War II, the US government made one of the smartest income-generating decisions they have ever made. Before the war, US citizens had to proactively pay taxes, similar to what I now do as a business owner. However, to pay for the war, rather than having taxpayers initiate their income tax payments every three months, the government took control.

On July 1, 1943, they began requiring employers to withhold taxes from the paychecks of employees across the nation.[1] This was brilliant for two key reasons:

1. **Income tax collection would be incredibly efficient.** The government would get a ton more money with less effort because they wouldn't have to chase down taxpayers' money. No more dealing with taxpayers who forgot or who were late with their payments. It was a set-it-and-forget-it method of collecting the income tax dollars.

2. **Taxpayers wouldn't notice as much.** Humans have a surprising ability to adapt and, after a little time, accept new norms. While you probably don't like seeing the income tax line item on your paycheck, you have most likely accepted it as "just how it is." In fact, it's likely that you don't even think about it much at all.

When I'm scrounging around for coins in my glove box to pay my 75¢ late fee because my local library still won't accept debit or credit cards,* I tend to think there isn't much to learn from how our government does things. But this is certainly one lesson we should learn from them. By making tax paying automatic, the government virtually guaranteed they would collect tax money quicker and with far less effort.

AUTOMATE FOR THE WIN

Let's face it. You and I are our own worst enemies when it comes to succeeding financially. Most of the time we know what to do. The

---

*   Nope, I am definitely not kidding. This happened to me just last week.

challenge is actually doing it. But what if success with money had nothing to do with willpower or self-discipline?

Successful people, in pretty much any sphere, seek to eliminate dependence on self-discipline whenever possible. And as much as possible, they try to make the most important tasks automatic.

Author James Clear explains it this way: "If you want better results, then forget about setting goals. Focus on your system instead. . . . You do not rise to the level of your goals. You fall to the level of your systems."[2]

This principle most certainly applies to our finances. People who are great with money don't have more self-discipline when it comes to making financial decisions. Rather, they set up systems to eliminate the need for self-discipline to consistently make good money choices.

Remember, financially successful people understand it isn't about willpower but is simply about making important financial decisions automatic or as simple as possible.

LINDA: I tend to feel guilty about being unorganized and undisciplined. But I've come to realize that it's not about being the most organized or disciplined—it's about automation. Whether you are a Monica or a Phoebe, you can set yourself up for success.

MONEY IS LIKE A CREEK

In my backyard we have a creek. When heavy rain falls up north, it fills to about six feet deep. And then a few days later, it's all but dried up.

I like to think of my money like that creek. Every month, money that I earn comes in and money that I spend goes out. It's all just passing through my hands. And when it's gone, it's gone.

When the water is high in that creek, I can easily grab a bucket and scoop out water. I can use it for watering my plants, washing my car, or anything else I need it for. But if I don't allocate it for specific tasks, then before I know it, it will be gone.

And an even better idea would be to automate the water distribution by digging a trench from that creek to my garden. Then every time the creek filled with water, it would automatically flow to my garden. I'd be able to grow fruit and vegetables without having to lift a finger.

We have the same opportunity to create trenches that automatically direct incoming money toward what is most important to us. And if we don't, like the water in the creek, it will just come in and go out and be gone.

SIMPLY AUTOMATE

When at all possible, find a way to do important financial tasks *automatically*. In everyday life, this could look like using your bank's bill-pay service to automatically send money on the first of the month to pay bills or give.

At a minimum, you can create a habit where giving becomes as close to automatic as possible. For example, on the first Sunday of the month, Linda and I give 10% to our church without fail.

Your Kick-Start

Want to jump ahead and complete your related challenge? Go to page 89 for details.

You could also use your bank's scheduled transfer feature to transfer money to a savings account. Each month, the amount you determine would move from your checking to your savings account, allowing you to automatically save up for your next vacation.

You could do the same with your retirement account by contributing to your 401(k) or 403(b) at work. Or set up a Roth IRA* that you

---

* For instructions on how to set up a Roth IRA, check out seedtime.com/roth.

automatically contribute to, or even make a college savings account for your kids. By doing so, you systematically and effortlessly begin moving toward financial goals that are important to you.

As a personal note of encouragement, I had read dozens of books about managing money before I began tapping into the power of financial automation. I kept pushing off this simple tweak (that could take as little as five minutes) because I didn't think it would make that big of a difference.

Trust me—this was a game changer for Linda and me. It seems like a small thing, but it really is huge. By making this one move, we instantly went from being hit-or-miss givers and savers to being 100% consistent. And with that consistency came tremendous growth in both areas as well.

So let me encourage you to actually do this. Don't wait until you've read a dozen other books telling you to do it. Do it now. Your future self will thank you.

CHAPTER 6

ADJUST: IF YOU FIND YOURSELF IN A HOLE, STOP DIGGING

My boss was one of the kindest guys I had ever met. He was a longtime executive who didn't take himself too seriously and was just as comfortable chatting with the peons like myself as he was with other executives. He was a shining example of what we all want a boss to be: fun, understanding, and kind. As a result, he got the best from his employees.

One Tuesday morning in 2007, he called the entire department into the conference room, which wasn't that unusual, but the fact that he wasn't smiling and making jokes was very odd. After the last of us had filed into the crammed conference room, he stepped in and slowly shut the door. When he turned toward us, I saw tears well up in his eyes.

As I sat there trying to figure out what was happening, he said, "Guys, there is no easy way to say this . . ." He proceeded to tell us that all 27 of us in that conference room would be without a job in just a few short months.

There is a lot more to this story that I'll get to in part 2 of this book, but suffice it to say that the months leading up to the layoff were scary. We were at the beginning of the Great Recession, and I knew our household income was going to drop by about 60%. Honestly, I had no idea whether my income would ever return to its previous level.

We prayed for God to move in our financial situation and meet our needs.[1] Even with the 60% income drop, we tried with all our might to follow the Never 100 Rule. While there were months we failed, I wanted to get as close as possible to never spending 100% of our income because I could sustain spending 105% of my income for a lot longer than spending 150%. So we adjusted everything downward to handle our new (and hopefully temporary) normal.

ADJUSTING YOUR SPENDING

I'll bet you're really good at adjusting your spending after you get a raise or land a big client or if business is going well. Linda has always considered herself one of the world's foremost experts at it.

For me, it used to go like this: My boss would say I would be getting a promotion and a raise. Then I would go home and tell Linda. She'd begin dancing around the room (high kicks and all) with a huge smile, brainstorming the fastest ways to spend our extra income. We would celebrate by going on vacation, buying that new dresser to replace the old one, buying new clothes, and maybe even upgrading the car so I could fit in with my new coworkers.

And inevitably, two months later, money felt tighter than it had before. This raise was supposed to create some breathing room. Why hadn't it? Because we quickly (too quickly, actually) adjusted our spending up to match our salary increase.

So why, when our income drops, are we so reluctant to adjust our spending down? Well, we all know why—it's just not fun, right?

But, in order to successfully follow the Never 100 Rule, we need to adjust our spending down if our income drops.

I'm sure you don't need any help when it goes up, so let's focus on when it goes down.

Now if your financial life is all rainbows and unicorns and you're crushing the Never 100 Rule already, then you can just scurry along to the next chapter. But if things ever change, you know what chapter to turn to.

IF YOU ARE UNEMPLOYED OR UNDEREMPLOYED

I know that a good number of people reading this book might be without income or without enough to make ends meet. If that is you, I want you to know I have been there. I know how incredibly challenging it can be. My best advice is to think of it like this:

Imagine you're in the middle of a lake, sitting in a canoe with multiple holes. Water begins filling the boat, and as soon as you realize what's happening, you try to stop the water at the source—the holes.

If there are six holes, you probably can't plug them all, but if you can plug two or three, you'll slow down the damage. And that may just be the difference between sinking and having enough time to row to shore and get on solid ground. In this situation, the goal isn't to solve the entire problem but simply to make it *less* bad.

You do what you can with what you can control, while praying and leaving to God what you can't control. Remember, no matter how bad it looks, God "is able to do exceedingly abundantly above all that we ask or think."[2]

THE SURVIVAL BUDGET

Over the past 15 years, we have had a few "opportunities" to adjust downward after huge drops in income. And each time we found ourselves with a massive income drop, I did the same exercise: I immediately created a survival budget.

It can often be done in as little as 10 minutes, but the benefits are huge. The goal is to see how little you can *temporarily* survive on. If you had to cut out every non-essential, how little could you live on?

So, I would grab my budget template and plug in all my expenses through the lens of the bare minimum needed.* Now, we all have our own definition of what *bare minimum* looks like, but in general, it should be only the absolutely essential items.

Simple Insight

For most people, food is the area with the most potential impact—from cutting back on eating out, to eliminating waste, to shopping at a cheaper grocery store, to using coupons. There is a lot of money to be saved when it comes to food.

As you go through the process, question every expense to see whether there is any way to eliminate or reduce it. For example, when we created our survival budget during that layoff, it had us eating solely at home, shopping at the cheapest grocery store, and avoiding snacky food. In addition, we cut pretty much all entertainment, reduced credit card payments to the monthly minimum, cut personal spending money down to almost nothing, and even considered selling a car to eliminate the car payment.

This might sound like an insane exercise. But it works. As you build your survival budget, remember these two key things:

1. Listing it out doesn't mean you'll live it. The goal is to find out how low you can go if you have to.

2. Even if you do have to live it, it's a *temporary* plan. It's not meant to last.

---

* Download my budget template for free at seedtime.com/budgeting.

	Normal Budget	Survival Budget	
Giving	$300	$300	Giving has never been negotiable for us.
Eating Out	$300	$0	Cut all eating out and only make food at home.
Groceries	$300	$400	Increase to cover cooking more. Shop at cheapest grocery store and avoid snacky food.
Entertainment	$100	$0	Pause all entertainment.
Transportation	$350	$350	If transportation is essential, then keep it. If not, cut non-essential expenses.
Coffee	$100	$20	Make coffee at home.
Cell Phone	$100	$100	
Fitness	$100	$0	Pause gym memberships and fitness classes, and work out at home.
Clothing	$150	$0	Pause clothing purchases.
Insurance	$250	$250	
Housing	$800	$800	
Retirement	$300	$0	Pause retirement savings.
Credit Card	$200	$100	Pay only the minimum payments required.
Monthly Total	**$3,350**	**$2,320**	
Annual Total	**$40,200**	**$27,840**	

One final point: When we talk about budgeting, this is pretty much the opposite of what we typically recommend. For your normal life, it's essential that your budget has non-essentials (aka fun stuff). That's what makes it work. But for this exercise, it is the opposite.

> **LINDA:** All right, so don't take this and go running to your spouse, saying, "This guy Bob just told me to stop eating out, cancel Netflix, and sell our car!" This is just an exercise, or if you happen to need to live it, then it's just a temporary solution. And remember, when used properly, it should bring relief, not panic.

FINDING HOPE IN THE DARKNESS

I've noticed that fear hides in the shadows. It thrives on ambiguity. But when you shine a light on it, it almost always is less intimidating. When you use this exercise, you're essentially shining a light on the worst-case scenario. It's one place I find encouragement amid the unknown.

During my layoff in 2008, after completing this exercise, we found that we could *survive* on about $2,300 a month. I concluded that, worst case, I could grab a job at the Starbucks down the road and easily pay our bills. Sure, it was a bad situation, but it helped to know exactly how little we needed to survive. This simple exercise opened our eyes, removed a lot of stress, and provided a dose of hope in a tough situation.

> **LINDA:** When Bob lost his job, my worst fears—getting evicted or having a car repossessed—came flooding in. Then Bob brought the numbers to me and spelled out reality, and it helped me see none of that would happen if we reduced our spending temporarily. The exercise of figuring out our survival budget calmed my fears because I could see the plan.

Remember, it's in the tough spots, when it doesn't look good, that we can watch God do miracles! Because we are in a position where we have to trust Him, our spirits have a chance to grow. And each time we've been there, He has done something we didn't see coming.

One time, it was an overflow of resources. One time, it took a while, but we continued to work hard and saw the fruit of perseverance in our lives and hearts. One time, there was money in our bank account, but we didn't know where it had come from. And you know Bob doesn't miss a beat, so this was a loaves-and-fishes miracle.

If you allow God to do His perfect work, you'll see fruit in your life that you can't get any other way.

CHAPTER 7

ACCOUNTABILITY: MAKE IT HARD
TO FAIL AND EASY TO SUCCEED

A few years ago, I was hiking through the mountains of Tennessee with four close friends. We were having a guys' weekend and doing what ambitious guys do—discussing some of our goals for the year—and we came up with a brilliant idea.

We had all done the "Will you be my accountability partner?" thing many times. We all knew what you probably know—that someone *saying* he is your accountability partner is almost always meaningless. You've been there before, right?

Nine times out of 10, those relationships don't help at all because there is no real consequence for failing. So we decided we were going to try something new. The experiment began with each of us picking a specific and measurable goal that we wanted to achieve in the next month.

I wanted to get back in the habit of working out, so for one month I committed to working out every day. We then took turns assigning a punishment to one another if we failed to stick with it. This is where it got really good. Because we knew one another really well, it was easy to create punishments that were sure to motivate us. I was having the best time coming up with punishments for the other guys, until it was my turn.

They knew I hadn't eaten fast food in well over a decade (with the obvious holy exception of Chick-fil-A) because I tend to be a pretty clean eater. Inspired by the documentary *Super Size Me* about what happens if you exclusively eat McDonald's for a month, they decided something along these lines would be fitting for me.

My punishment would be that if I failed to work out every day for the entire month, I would have to eat *every single meal* at McDonald's for one week.

> LINDA: When I heard about this, I said, "Absolutely not. No way are you doing that! You'll be sick all week, and I am not going to parent alone because you lost a lousy bet."

As terrifying as the thought of failing was, I knew that this was going to *ensure* that I didn't fail. But what if I did? There was no way they would let me off the hook.

Once the trip ended and I got back home, the reality of this commitment began to sink in. It's fairly easy to work out three days a week, but it's immensely more difficult to go 31 consecutive days without missing a workout.

The first week wasn't too bad. I thought, *I can do this.* The next week, we were traveling, and things became a little tricky. One night I had to go to a hole-in-the-wall "gym" at 11 p.m. while completely exhausted.

The third week was insanely cold (in January), and all I wanted to do was sit by the fireplace. I definitely didn't want to work out. But I really didn't want a weeklong diet of Big Macs, so I did it anyway.

The final week was the hardest of all. I got sick. I don't recall whether it was the flu or what; all I remember is dragging myself out of bed to get my workout in for the day. I hated every minute of it, but compared with the punishment, it was absolutely worth it.

> LINDA: Normally, I would have told him to stay in bed, but with that awful punishment looming over our heads, I told him, "You think you feel bad now? Guess how bad you'll

feel if you have to eat McDonald's for a week! Just get it over with."

For the first time in my life, I had real accountability. No matter how I felt, where I was, or anything else, I persisted. The crazy plan worked. By God's grace, I made it the whole month, which certainly wouldn't have happened were it not for true accountability (aka seven days of Big Macs).

ACCOUNTABILITY AND MONEY

When you think of accountability and your money, you probably assume having a budget is the key. And you would be right—kind of. Let me explain.

I've spent more than 13 years personally testing different budgeting methods. I'm a money nerd like that. I must have tried dozens of apps, tools, and approaches. God bless Linda as I dragged her along on the journey of constantly experimenting with them all.

But I was saddened to discover that every method had the same problem: it was easy to cheat. Maybe you've been there too. Linda and I would create a budget by carefully assigning each dollar to a spending category. Our spending would be limited to the amount of money in any given category. If we overspent, the numbers would go red, but it was easy to ignore the red or explain it away. It was a veil of accountability—not a real deterrent. None of the budgeting methods we tried provided *real* accountability.

Without any significant deterrent, we followed the path of least resistance. In the case of money, that meant spending all we had until a real barrier made us stop. We needed a wall.

THE ONE-CATEGORY BUDGET

Have you ever heard of the 80/20 rule? It was birthed out of the observation that 80% of the effects often come from just 20% of the actions. For example, many businesses find that 80% of their sales come from just 20% of their products.

I was curious to see how this pattern played out with our blog, so I ran some numbers. Turns out, 80% of our traffic came from just 20% of our blog posts. Then I started looking at our money management and budgeting. Was the same pattern present there too? I mean, what if we could get 80% of the results of budgeting while doing only 20% of the work?

As I looked at our personal finances and began evaluating the progress of some of our students, I was thrilled to see this 80/20 pattern in action. About 20% of our budgeting efforts yielded about 80% of the results. This discovery led me to begin pointing new and failed budgeters to what we call the One-Category Budget.

You start by identifying the one area of your spending that is toughest to rein in. For most people, this tends to be one of the following:

- eating out
- groceries
- random Amazon purchases
- clothing
- entertainment
- hobbies

Simple Insight

If you aren't sure which area this is for you, then just follow the guidance in chapter 4 about paying attention to be able to accurately identify it.

Ask yourself which area of spending is hardest to control. This area will become your One-Category Budget, your focal point—the one category you're actually trying to control. As you do, you'll get the most reward for your effort.

Let's look at an example. Jerry is struggling to rein in his grocery purchases. He wants to spend $500 a month but consistently finds himself spending $600 or $700 a month. He can choose one of these three options:

1. **Open a separate checking account only for that category.** At the beginning of the month, Jerry would transfer $500 from his main checking to this new account and buy only groceries with this new debit card.

2. **Buy a reloadable gift card for that category.** At the beginning of the month, Jerry would buy a reloadable gift card from his local grocery store and put $500 on it. He would then refill it each month when he gets paid and buy only groceries with this card.

3. **Pull cash out to be used only for that category.** At the beginning of the month when Jerry gets paid, he would pull out $500 cash and that is all he can spend on groceries until next month.

With any of these three options, Jerry is far more likely to stay on track with his grocery spending. In addition, by focusing on the one category he consistently overspends in, Jerry is putting the least amount of effort into budgeting but generating the most savings.

When you create walls and a hard stop for your spending in one category, it provides much better accountability than just seeing red numbers on a budgeting app when you overspend. Additionally, this approach is great because you aren't focusing any time or energy on the categories that aren't going to make much of a difference. Rather, you focus only on the one category that will have the most impact.

Less work, more results. That's what I love best. The One-Category Budget is the quickest and best on-ramp to controlling your spending that I have ever seen.[*]

Your KICK-START

Want to jump ahead and complete your related challenge? Go to page 90 for details.

If you are already budgeting and have a method that is working, great! Stick with what works for you. But if you don't budget or you need a new approach, then try out the One-Category Budget. It will help you get close to 80% of the results with about 20% of the work.

But the bottom line is that you need to find some approach to managing your money that actually holds you accountable and makes it hard to fail and easy to succeed. With true accountability in place, we can be the type of people who, regardless of our income levels, save money, give generously, and prepare for the future.

[*]   To find our accountability solution for a full budget, check out our Real Money Method training at seedtime.com/real.

CHAPTER 8

HOW TO SPEND MORE ON
WHAT YOU LOVE

Ever since he was a little boy, Brandon had loved airplanes. His mom would take him to the airport to watch the planes, and his dad would build model planes with him. He always dreamed of learning how to fly.

Over the years, his dream seemed to drift further out of his reach. Between a mortgage, student loans, and an unexpected surgery, he couldn't seem to ever save money. Something was always in the way.

One day he started tracking his spending (just like we talked about in chapter 4). Through this exercise, Brandon noticed something unexpected. He and his wife were paying $150 a month on cable TV, plus an additional $20 a month on streaming services.

They had always paid for cable because they thought it was just what everyone does. Once they started thinking about it, they realized that almost everything they watched was on Netflix. Then Brandon discovered that he could take flying lessons—like he had always dreamed—for about $150 an hour.

The next day, he called the cable company and canceled his subscription. The $150 he saved went directly to a special account for flight lessons. A couple of months later, Brandon sat behind the yoke during his first flight lesson, overflowing with excitement. A childhood dream had been within reach all along. It merely required him to declutter his spending by cutting something he didn't care about so he could focus on something he did.

Smart spending doesn't mean deprivation and penny-pinching. Rather, smart spending gives you the freedom to pursue a rich life by focusing on what you love most. What if you could spend guilt-free on the things you love? What would you be willing to give up so you could make it happen?

> Smart spending gives you the freedom to pursue a rich life by focusing on what you love most.

WHAT DO YOU LOVE MOST?

The first step in decluttering is to determine those things that you absolutely love. Imagine having an endless supply of funds. Where would you be spending your money? Maybe you love decorating your house, traveling, photography, or seeing movies at the theater. Or do you love new clothes, reading, coffee, or eating out?

Use the space below to list things you love but don't spend much on because there never seems to be enough money left.

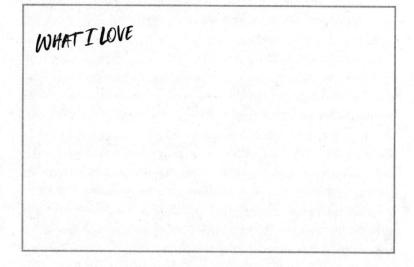

WHAT I LOVE

Once you have this clear, it's time to think about eliminating the clutter in your spending. Remember, the money you spend each month on stuff that you don't really need or care about is *wasted money*. Instead, this money should be put toward things that are truly important to you.

Maybe you're always ordering from DoorDash or Uber Eats when you would be just as content with a frozen dinner. Maybe you have a habit of going on a vacation every year even though travel stresses you out.

Some people are fanatical about their cars. Others view cars just as a means to get from point A to B. If you're the A to B type, use it to your advantage. While it might be nice to have a newer car, if it doesn't excite you, then focus on something that does. Sell it, and get something reliable, in great shape, and a lot cheaper. Don't waste money on the things you don't value, regardless of what experts or others around you say.

> **LINDA:** If you like playing golf or getting doughnuts every Saturday, then allow yourself that freedom! Freedom to spend on what you love. Let that benefit outweigh the minor inconvenience of changing how you spend on the stuff you care less about.

I know what you might be thinking: *Bob, every dollar I spend is on necessities and things important to me.* Maybe that's true. But it's far more likely that some of the things you buy each month are more important to you than others. Financial author Ramit Sethi calls these "Money Dials." He explains,

> *It's OK to recognize that you have areas you naturally love and want to spend on. What others think of your spending doesn't matter because everyone has different Money Dials. It's simply a matter of different priorities! In other words, what you value will be different from what others value. If you LOVE to spend your*

money on week-long trips to exotic locales every week, but some-one else would rather spend that same amount of money on hav-ing the latest iPhone, then that's great—and perfectly normal!

It's just being true and honest to ourselves and what our Money Dials are. . . .

Not only will we have more money and energy to spend on the things that bring us happiness, but we'll be able to spend on those things guilt-free, since we know we've freed up the money by ig-noring everything else.

It's intimidating and liberating at the same time. It allows us to say, "Hey, this is important to me—and that's not."¹

LINDA: And if you're married, be sure you consider what you both want and need to spend money on. There is a constant give-and-take for Bob and me on what is more important, but we both definitely have our say.

Now it's your turn. What are you spending money on that's not im-portant to you? Use the space below to list or draw the clutter in your spending. What can you eliminate so you can spend more on what you love?

CLUTTER TO REMOVE

If you're thinking, *I don't have anything to put here. I love all the things I buy,* then fast-forward to the first challenge on page 88 to start tracking your spending. I've found that seeing my spending in black and white often highlights my spending clutter.

PICK YOUR HOBBIES STRATEGICALLY

When I was 13 years old, I spent every dollar I earned on golf. I would play two or three times a week and became a pretty good golfer for my age. While I liked golf, it was never really my favorite sport. But my identity had become wrapped up in it, so I kept playing. It was what I and others had come to expect.

As I got older, it dawned on me that spending all my money on a hobby just because I had an aptitude for it or because it was what I was known for didn't make much sense. So, even though it wasn't easy, I laid down that part of my identity.

Additionally, over the years, I began better aligning my hobbies with my goals by asking these questions:

- What if I chose hobbies that weren't inherently expensive?
- What if I chose hobbies that could make me healthier?
- What if I chose hobbies that would generate income?

When I started asking these questions, I began to see hobbies in a different light. Instead of paying $50 a round to play golf, I could play tennis for free, spend less on equipment, and get better exercise.

Instead of my childhood obsession with bonsai trees (no idea where this came from—maybe *The Karate Kid*?), I could focus on vegetable gardening. It would give me better exercise and create food that was healthier than what's in the grocery store.

What if I didn't have to spend over 500 hours a year watching all 162 St. Louis Cardinals games? What if I used some of that time to create an eBay hobby where I get the thrill of winning when I sell something? Instead of the thrill of victory being based on something that is out of my control (the Cardinals), it's now based on something that I have some control over and that yields monetary benefit.

Now, I'm not saying we should lay down the things we truly love. Instead, let's honestly and intentionally identify them. And let's ask questions to see whether a hobby is truly something we love or something we continue because our identity is wrapped up in it. It's okay to lay a hobby down and do something new.

LINDA: I literally laughed out loud when I read the title of this section. If you know Bob at all, you know he wants everything in his life to be as efficient as possible. He once told me he didn't like watching sad movies because it was an inefficient use of his time. I nearly fell off my chair.

At first, this point seemed just a funny reminder of his personality. As I read on, though, I started to see things in a new light. Don't get me wrong—I'm not going to stop loving the things I love because they're not efficient. But now I'm asking myself whether I've been wasting money on things because of a lack of creativity on my part.

So, I'm asking you to open your mind and see if, by chance, you've been missing out on a golden opportunity because you just didn't see it before.

USE FRICTION TO STEER SPENDING

Now that you've identified the things you love, it's time to declutter your spending. You can use friction to your advantage to help ensure that every dollar you spend is intentional rather than impulsive. Make it slightly more difficult to spend on the things you don't want and easier to spend on the things you want.

In his book, *Atomic Habits,* James Clear says this:

> *People often choose products not because of what they are, but because of where they are. If I walk into the kitchen and see a plate of cookies on the counter, I'll pick up half a dozen and start eating, even if I hadn't been thinking about them beforehand and didn't necessarily feel hungry. If the communal table at the office is always filled with doughnuts and bagels, it's going to be hard not to grab one every now and then. Your habits change depending on the room you are in and the cues in front of you.*
>
> *Environment is the invisible hand that shapes human behavior.* [2]

These nudges are all around us, from the placement of items on grocery store shelves to preinstalled software on our devices. Our decisions are being influenced—often far more drastically than we realize—by seemingly insignificant nudges. So, if marketers are trying to nudge us toward spending, let's set up some roadblocks to help minimize it. Here are a few suggestions:

- Hide (or delete) any apps that you regularly buy from on your mobile devices.

- Unsubscribe from retailer mailing lists (both online and off-line). Yes, you might miss that 10%-off coupon, but by not seeing it, you'll save far more.

- Stop following particular brands or people on social media that lead to frivolous spending.

- Create a rule where you purchase from Amazon only one day a week. Oftentimes if you just wait until the next day, the craving for the item subsides.

- Here's a tough one. Delete your credit card information from Amazon and other online retailers so you have to enter it manually each time you buy.

If you're like me, you probably think these ideas are annoying and will take away some fun. You're right—they can. But like a tiny rudder on a ship, little additions of friction will steer us in the direction of our desires so we don't just drift mindlessly with the current. Remember, the goal is to spend *more on the things you love* by using friction to spend *less on the things you like.* Say no to the good in order to be able to say yes to the great.

> LINDA: I've learned that telling your spouse what expenses you plan to cut is a bad idea. Remember, you didn't get married to rule over your spouse. Even if you handle the money alone, your spouse is your partner. Don't forget to treat him or her like one.
>
> A friend gave me the best advice on speaking with someone I love about a tricky situation, especially when I know I'm right. "Go to them with the most humility you can muster," she said. The goal is to keep the relationship solid, not to get what you want. Try something like this: "Hey, so our finances are just not where I think either of us wants them. I'm thinking about creating a plan so we can make some progress. How do you feel about that?"
>
> Ask your spouse what he or she would like to be able to spend more money on. Does he or she want to go on a

family vacation each year? To fund a certain ministry or organization? To get a monthly massage? Whatever it is, you can use it to get your spouse on board. And not only that, but you'll also be on the same page and able to make both your dreams come true.

CHAPTER 9

HOW TO SPEND SMARTER
(AND THE BUBBLE TAURUS)

Right after Linda and I got married, I found out my little sister was going to trade in her 12-year-old Taurus to get a newer car. The dealer was going to give her only $1,000 for it, so I asked her to sell it to me instead. Here's why:

At the time, Linda and I worked day jobs on opposite sides of town. We drove about 20 miles to work each day and really needed two reliable forms of transportation. We had two cars, but both were having more and more issues.

While we didn't need a third car at that moment, if one of our vehicles did have a major issue, I knew I'd have to make one of two choices: either race to find a loan and buy a new car or pay for major repairs, which would likely cost more than the value of either car.

I estimated we would have to borrow (at a minimum) $5,000 to get something that fit our needs. Adding to the stress, we would need to replace the vehicle with something else immediately—since Uber wasn't around yet. I concluded that if I bought my sister's car, then I would be paying $1,000 for an insurance policy of sorts to prevent bigger costs down the road.

Simple INSiGHT

Whenever possible, you want to try to avoid having to make quick decisions on major purchases. Patience always yields better deals.

Additionally, my sister's Taurus was a good car. She had performed regular maintenance and it ran great. I reasoned that if I had to buy a car in a few months, then I would be hard pressed to find one as well taken care of as hers. Plus, I knew that driving a 12-year-old, bubble-looking Taurus would make me irresistible to my brand-new wife. Right, honey?

LINDA: Hmmmm. No comment, dear.

I didn't see much downside (except that Linda hated that car).

> **LINDA:** Well, hate is a strong word, but . . .

I figured that even if a couple of years went by and I never needed it, I could probably sell it for close to what I paid for it, because it was so far down the depreciation curve (more on that in a minute). So, with that, my sister sold me her legendary bubble Taurus for $1,000.

Wouldn't you know it? Within months, the engine blew on my car, leaving me with repairs that cost far more than the car was worth. I sold it to the mechanic at the car repair shop and started cruising around in my bubble Taurus.

I'm not going to lie. It was tough pushing away all the fawning women as I drove around town in that bubble for the next few years. For the first time, I had a glimpse of what it was like to be in Bieber's shoes.

> **LINDA:** Last time I checked, Bieber was wearing Crocs.

Unlike Justin, it took me a couple of years to save up enough to buy our next car with cash, and as soon as we did, I traded in that old Taurus. Guess how much we got for it?

$1,000. Boom.

> **LINDA:** When Bob told me he wanted to buy his sister's car, I'm pretty sure I said something to the effect of "Can I just have that $1,000 instead?" I honestly thought this was a waste and we'd never need it. But I had to eat my words when it actually paid off. And that really did make him irresistible!

And for the car lovers out there who are offended by the thought of driving a car that old, I'm someone who generally views cars as a tool to get from point A to B. So driving around in a bubble Taurus was simply a means of spending less on the things I didn't care much about so I could spend more on what mattered most to me like we talked about in the previous chapter.*

Wouldn't you know? I drove that bubble Taurus around for over four years, never had a car payment, and sold it for what I paid for it. If there were a *SportsCenter* highlight reel for financial wins, this should have been on it! Now I know this is an extreme example, but it makes an important point. Exploiting the depreciation curve can save us tons of money.

MYTH: ONLY NEW CARS ARE RELIABLE

I grew up believing that as soon as your car hit 100,000 miles, you had to get a new one because it was basically a ticking time bomb that was going to leave you stranded on the side of the road with major repairs. Automotive journalist Doug DeMuro debunks this myth: "It used to be, back in the 1960s and 70s, that cars weren't really expected to get past 100,000 miles. . . . Even as cars started to improve in the 1980s and 1990s, many car shoppers still had this 100,000-mile cutoff forever emblazoned in their minds. . . . Only in the past decade or so have people finally started to realize that when properly maintained, many cars can hit 200,000 miles. Some can hit 300,000 miles."[1]

When we got married, we drove our Honda Fit (which basically had a lawn-mower-sized engine) to over 150,000 miles without a single problem. I'm convinced that whoever is driving that car will drive it way beyond 200,000 miles.

The only reason we traded it in was to get a Honda Pilot, which was better equipped for our growing family. We

---

* As promised, this isn't theory for me. I live this stuff!

drove it for over 250,000 miles without any major engine or transmission issues before needing another upgrade to better accommodate our kid situation. If you buy a reliable car (this is key) and take reasonable care of it, you should have no problem safely driving it well beyond the 100,000-mile mark.

Here are a few more realizations that helped me break out of the new-car-every-two-or-three-years cycle:

1. *Cars now are less likely to leave you stranded.*[2] Our vehicles are far more advanced than ever before. While these advancements come with new complications, the fact is that today's cars are less likely to leave you stranded on the side of the road.

2. *We have cell phones.* No one wants to be broken down on the side of the road. But for 99% of us, it's far less terrifying than it was 50 years ago, when you might have had to wave down a passing driver or walk up to a stranger's house to use the phone.

3. *We have Uber.* Even if you can't get ahold of a friend to come pick you up, you can probably have an Uber picking you up in 10 minutes or so.

We're blessed to live in the 21st century, and the "risks" of driving an older car simply aren't what they were just a few decades ago. But far too many people are still making buying decisions based on those fears that their parents had of a car breaking down and being stranded.

Most people don't want to drive a beater, but the good news is, you still don't have to trade your car in every three years for a new one. When you begin looking, you'll find tons of cars that are 5 to 10 years old that look new, are super reliable, and cost a quarter of what newer cars cost.

Changing your mindset about how you buy cars is, for most people, the best money-saving strategy you'll find. If you can break out of the new-car-every-few-years cycle by driving a reliable car for longer, you have the opportunity to easily save many thousands of dollars each year.

THE DEPRECIATION CURVE

For those new to this term, depreciation is simply the reduction in something's value over time. You know how everyone says a new car goes down in value by more than $1,000 the minute you drive it off the lot? That's depreciation, my friend.

You can think of it like a silent killer eroding the value of most things we own.

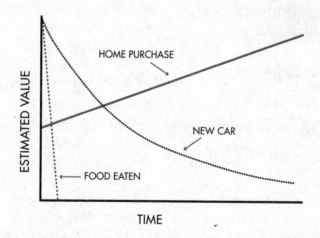

Let's say you go to a restaurant. You order the fish tacos because—well, it's obvious. You pay $15 for them, and they're worth every penny. How much are they worth after you gobble them down? $0, right? Sadly, you can never eat those tacos again; you'll have to buy more. Once eaten, they lose all their value.

Or if you buy a new $20,000 car today and want to sell it tomorrow, you'll be lucky to get $19,000 for it. Three years later, it might be worth $12,000. And eventually, like my old bubble Taurus, the depreciation will slow so much that you might be able to buy and sell at the same price.

Now let's say you buy a house. While real estate doesn't always appreciate—and there are times when the market tanks—more often than not, real estate tends to increase in value.

The point is that a dollar spent on any item will be worth widely varying amounts in one month, one year, and 10 years. By spending less on things that depreciate, we have the opportunity to *invest* in items that appreciate—and this is the key to increasing our AUM and building wealth.

> By spending less on things that depreciate, we have the opportunity to *invest* in items that appreciate—and this is the key to increasing our AUM and building wealth.

Just being aware of this is incredibly important. Because then you can factor it into your buying decisions. This is why I am always asking the question, *What will this be worth a year from now?* It's constantly on a loop in my head. I know—I told you I'm a weirdo. The good news is that you can begin asking this question and prioritizing your spending even if you're living paycheck to paycheck.

For most of us in the lower and middle classes, we don't have the option to spend 80% of our income on real estate and investments that will grow. But we do have the ability to buy things that depreciate slower, which is one of the easiest and most effective ways to begin increasing your AUM.

> **LINDA:** Again, the point isn't to *never* buy things that depreciate. That's unrealistic and crazy! We have to buy them. However, when possible, just try to buy things that depreciate slower. Every time we do, we're adding money to our future pockets, and though we may not see the benefits instantly, they're definitely coming. And they'll be well worth it.

Now, don't throw the book down because you think I'm telling you to buy only old stuff. I'm not. My goal is for you to walk away with an understanding of how to exploit the depreciation curve to your advantage and prioritize your spending accordingly. Another way to do this is to choose total value over price.

THINK TOTAL VALUE RATHER THAN PRICE

When we focus only on the price of an item, we tend to be thinking short term. On the other hand, when we look at the total value of an item, we're thinking long term—we look past its surface to see its value now and over time.

Of course, sometimes that means spending more on the front end. For example, for the past 15 years, I've used only Apple products. Apple generally makes reliable products, but I am even more interested in the fact that they tend to hold their value better than their competitors'.

So when I'm done with the phone, laptop, or watch, I know that I can go to eBay and get a pretty good price for it, especially compared to the alternatives.

Simple Insight

Some of the best values can be found in buying *used* items from sought-after brands. In many cases, you can buy a better product for considerably less than the new item from a no-name brand. Plus, the name-brand product often maintains its value better than other brands, so it's worth more a few years down the road.

HOW DO YOU KNOW WHAT DEPRECIATES SLOWER?

Depreciation data often isn't readily available, so one of my favorite ways to get a feel for an item's long-term value (i.e., whether it depreciates slower than alternatives) is to look at eBay. It's the world's biggest marketplace of used goods and can reveal the current true value of many items. Here is how to determine the value of a particular item:

1. Open ebay.com.

2. Click "Advanced Search."

3. Check the "Sold Listings" box.

4. Search for the item.

From here you can see the exact prices that the item has sold for recently. You can scroll through and quickly get a feel for what it's actually worth. This works for almost anything you can imagine. There are certainly exceptions, but it's the best way I have found to determine an item's true worth.

You can apply this total-value focus to a variety of areas, but where this makes the most impact is with cars. Thankfully, a lot of this information is compiled already and available for free online. Edmunds.com has what it calls a TCO (True Cost to Own) number for a wide variety of cars.

The TCO factors in depreciation, insurance premiums, maintenance and repair costs, taxes and fees, and fuel costs. All this data is presented as one number, which lets you easily compare three or four vehicles.

For example, if you were to compare a 2020 Ford Fusion and a 2020 Honda Civic, at surface level they cost about the same. However, when you look at the TCO number, there is a $3,841 difference. Through this analysis, we can see that owning the Civic will be $3,841 cheaper than owning the Fusion over the next five years.[3]

2020 Fusion SE Four-Door Sedan (1.5L 4cyl Turbo 6A)		2020 Civic Sport Four-Door Sedan (2.0L 4cyl CVT)	
Insurance	$3,941	Insurance	$4,000
Maintenance	$3,509	Maintenance	$3,394
Repairs	$792	Repairs	$612
Taxes and Fees	$1,860	Taxes and Fees	$1,624
Financing	$4,176	Financing	$4,154
Depreciation	$11,909	Depreciation	$9,486
Fuel	$5,904	Fuel	$4,980
True Cost to Own	$32,091	True Cost to Own	$28,250
Purchase Price	$22,970	Purchase Price	$22,851

If all other factors are equal and I can't decide which car to choose, I'd go with the one that will save me $3,841 in the years to come!*

Simple INSight

At the time of this writing, Toyota, Lexus, Subaru, and Honda tend to hold their value better than their competitors. You might end up paying more on the front end, but when you go to sell the car, you'll likely sell it faster and for considerably more than the alternatives.

NOT EVERY DECISION IS A FINANCIAL ONE

It's important to mention that money isn't the only consideration in a buying decision. Money spent on a vacation depreciates very quickly, but the benefit from the rest and memories is an important factor to consider.

Or in the case of reading a book (like this one), the value is not in the actual object but in how it changes you. In my case, numerous books have yielded 100 times more than what I paid for the book. And hopefully, this book does the same for you.

LINDA: You want to know what I thought when I first read this chapter? *Depreciating assets can really make life fun!* And it's true. They really do. My problem was that my fun could tend toward foolishness. It's important to have a healthy balance. Don't squander your money, but also, life is meant to be lived. Depending on your personality

---

* Next time you're shopping for a car, run a comparison yourself at edmunds.com/tco .html.

type, you need to hear one of those two things. I need reminders not to squander my money, and Bob tends to need more inspiration to live a little. Which is surely why God knew that we needed each other. We're MFEO (name that movie!).*

EXTRA CREDIT: BUY THINGS THAT GROW

One of the most important financial lessons I ever learned is this: every dollar spent is going to either increase or decrease in value. It seems obvious and simple. Yet so few see the profound power of letting this principle guide how they spend their money.

We've spent most of this chapter focusing on things that decrease in value like cars, electronics, and food. Reducing the amount we lose to depreciation is often a huge—and overlooked—opportunity for financial progress.

But if you really want to see your AUM grow, start spending your money on things that don't depreciate at all but instead have a high likelihood of increasing in value over time. Here are a few ways to do so:

- pay extra toward your mortgage
- contribute to a 401(k), 403(b), or Roth IRA
- invest in crowdfunded real estate†
- invest in index funds, mutual funds, large cap stocks, or bonds
- simply add to a savings account

---

*   Where are my *Sleepless in Seattle* fans?

†   The two I currently use are fundrise.com and diversyfund.com. For more on these or more in-depth investing training to grow your AUM faster, visit seedtime.com/investing.

Simple Insight

Automate investing in things that grow (like we talked about in chapter 5). Set up your bank account to automatically pull out $100 to put toward savings or another investment account. That's $100 less in your spending account to use on an impulsive Amazon purchase, which would have likely depreciated quickly.

There is a tendency to see small steps like these as insignificant. Don't believe that lie. I love how Zechariah puts it: "Do not despise these small beginnings, for the LORD rejoices to see the work begin."[4]

So begin asking yourself with each dollar you spend, *How much will this be worth in a year?* By getting in this habit, you'll start to see how much you spend on things that are taking money out of your pocket. And remember, even when you can't spend on something that grows, buy something that depreciates slower.

CHAPTER 10

THE HIDDEN EXPERIMENT
WE'RE ALL PART OF

I magine leaving your house and driving to a quaint café. You're greeted at the door; then you sit down and open the menu. There are four choices. Yes, four. And you are allowed to order only one item off the small menu.

Now imagine a restaurant with an endless all-you-eat buffet. Grab as many plates as you'd like. As far as your eye can see, every type of food you can imagine is sitting right in front of you. Oh, and if you want, it can be delivered to your home—no need to drive anywhere to get it.

This is essentially what happened with the introduction of the credit card in the 1950s. Average consumers went from being relatively limited on the things they could buy with credit to essentially having no limits with what we can buy on credit. So just like at that all-you-can-eat buffet, there is a good chance you'll eat more than you should. And, well, you can see where this is going, right?

For the past 60 or so years, we have been part of what I call the easy-credit experiment, an experiment that has massively hindered our ability to live within our means.

THE RESULTS OF THE EXPERIMENT

The first credit card as we know it came out in the late 1950s, and while the concept of credit and debt has been around for thousands

of years, everything changed with the credit card.[1] Before its introduction, people borrowed money to buy a house, a car, maybe a
horse. They were limited, though, because they could get a loan only
from the merchant selling that particular item.

But somewhere in the 1950s, banks began this experiment by asking, "What if we could lend people money to buy *anything* they
wanted?"

And look at what happened.

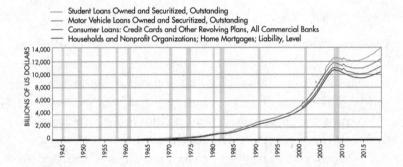

US consumers went from virtually zero household debt in the
1950s to over $14 trillion in 2021.[2] Just for fun, here's what $14 trillion
looks like:

$14,000,000,000,000.

The US went from basically no household debt to that. In just a
few generations.

THE LIE THAT FOLLOWED

If we look at the easy-credit experiment as a whole, it has been a
runaway success. For the banks, anyway. And since credit cards have
been the key player in this experiment, it's easy to look at them as
the most destructive piece of this puzzle.

But I don't believe credit cards are the most damaging part. I believe the most destructive result of this experiment is far more sub-tle: *the belief that debt is normal.* That taking on massive amounts of debt is just "what you do" in the 21st century. This belief has been so commonly accepted that 86% of millennials in the US are in debt.[3]

The danger in this simple little lie is that if debt is normal—something everyone does—then it becomes *necessary.* Taking on massive amounts of debt becomes the *only* way to live in the 21st century. But this was never God's intention for us.

> **LINDA:** I would add to "debt is normal" the other lie that "image is everything." We feel like we must have the newest and best because that's what everyone else is doing.
>
> Several years ago, I was shopping with my sister when she found something she liked. My first instinct as the amazing shopping partner that I am (for real, I have references) was to say, "Oh, you should get it! Try it on!"
>
> To which she replied, "Well, it's not gonna happen today." I assumed that money was tight for her, so she needed to say no. Immediately I felt sympathy and told her I was sorry.
>
> She shrugged and said, "Eh, I'm the same without it."
>
> My eyes opened wide, and I thought, *She's the same without it!*
>
> I let those words soak into my very being. Now, years later, I repeat them to myself as a reminder that I'm not the sum of all the stuff I own. My worth is found in one place.
>
> If I'm searching for it in a new wardrobe or the latest tech gadget or whatever, then I'll never ever be satisfied. But when I see myself as fully known yet fully loved, that new shirt doesn't matter so much. It's just for fun and not for validation.

THE OTHER MASTER

Jesus didn't come to this earth to break us free from the bondage of sin, only for us to be enslaved in debt to another master.

Author Craig Hill explains it this way:

> *If God personally appeared in physical form in our church and asked us as a congregation to participate financially in a missions project, most people couldn't do so, whether they wanted to or not. One hundred percent of their monthly cash flow is already allocated to their debt obligations. So in reality they can't obey The Master because they have many other "masters" who must be satisfied first.[4]*

When we're slaves to debt, we're not fully free to follow God's leading. Debt can and often does hinder our ability to be used by God.

A pastor friend of mine told a story of a congregant in his church who felt called to work on his church staff. They both felt good about moving forward, but as my friend shared the base pay rate for the position, the prospective employee broke down crying. He went on to communicate how many thousands of dollars he owed each month in debt repayments. As much as he knew he was called to the position, he concluded it would be impossible for him to take the pay cut to work in ministry.

> Jesus didn't come to this earth to break us free from the bondage of sin, only for us to be enslaved in debt to another master.

I've heard countless stories like this. Where people are called by God—their true master—but because they are beholden to so many other masters with their debt, they feel as if they can't do what God has called them to do.

THE ROOT OF THE PROBLEM

God can't keep you out of debt. I know that sounds like a bold statement, but barring the elimination of our free will, He simply can't do it. No matter how many times God supernaturally pulls us out of debt, because we have free will, we can fall back into old habits, spend more than we have, and get right back into debt. We must fix the root cause of our debt so we can climb out and stay out.

Have you ever met anyone who prayed to lose 20 pounds, then woke up the next day 20 pounds lighter? Me neither. Could God make that happen? Sure, but I think we all know that when we pray to lose weight, He most likely is going to help us make the lifestyle changes that will lead to the weight loss.

And while you might get a check in the mail to pay off all your debt (and I hope you do!), I think it's more likely that God is going to help you make changes to your lifestyle that will lead to debt freedom.

A SHOEBOX FULL OF SECRETS

Shortly after Linda said yes to my marriage proposal, we began to get *real* real with each other. And so when we sat down to talk about our money situation, she handed me a shoebox. Hmmm. At that point we were both in pretty sketchy financial situations, but I didn't know the extent of her situation. And I had no idea what was packed tightly inside this shoebox.

What could be inside? Maybe it was full of $100 bills and this was her way of saying, "Baby, this is my dowry. Where do you want to go on our honeymoon?"

Maybe it was a puppy? That would be fun. Kind of.

When I removed the lid, I saw a stack of envelopes. Not quite as fun. Upon further inspection, I discovered that they all had a credit card name attached: Citibank, Discover, and Chase. Pretty much the opposite of a box full of $100 bills. This began our first real chat about money as we shared the skeletons in our closets (or shoeboxes).

In this tell-all conversation, we both revealed all the debt we would bring into the marriage. Then we committed, as a team, to pay off these debts. It was no longer her debt and my debt but *our* debt.

> **LINDA:** This was my first lesson in dealing with my finances guilt-free. I had been so ashamed of how chaotic my money situation had gotten that I was scared to show Bob my mess. But when I did, I realized that even though he was laughing at my shoebox "filing system," I wasn't alone. We could join forces to fix this. I was so thankful and relieved that I no longer had to be governed by shame but could walk in the freedom that love gives.

THE DEBT SNOWBALL

It can be hard to see past the mountain of debt and easy to feel crushed. While sometimes it can seem insurmountable, with God's grace we can overcome any obstacle—including a mountain of debt. One of the most practical approaches for paying off debt—and my go-to recommendation—is the Debt Snowball.

Simply put, you pay off debts in the order of smallest to largest balances rather than highest to lowest interest rates. To numbers nerds like myself, paying off highest interest rates first makes the most sense. But the snowball approach prioritizes more frequent milestones. And studies have proved the effectiveness of this method over the alternatives.[5]

It is a wonderful feeling to be able to celebrate your first milestone—paying off the first debt is so satisfying! But if you focus on the highest interest rate, it could be many months or even years before you reach that first milestone. Would you have the endurance to keep going that long without some tangible encouragement? We definitely didn't! But by prioritizing milestones, even small goals, you're essentially acting as your own cheerleader.

To implement the Debt Snowball, you start by paying only the minimum payment on all debts, except the one with the smallest balance (we'll call it debt A). Pay as much as possible toward debt A. After you pay it off, take everything you were paying toward debt A and put all that financial energy toward the next smallest debt. Continue that process down the list of debts. With each payoff, the payments get larger and the momentum begins building like a snowball, hence the name.*

If you have $300 extra available to pay toward debt each month . . .

Debts	Balance	Minimum Payment	How Much to Pay This Month?
Debt A	$1,000	$100	100+300=$400
Debt B	$4,000	$250	$250
Debt C	$3,000	$50	$50

---

* We created a plug-and-play Debt Snowball worksheet that we'd love to give you. If you need it, just go to seedtime.com/snowball to get your copy.

Once debt A is paid off, start working on debt C.

Debts	Balance	Minimum Payment	How Much to Pay This Month?
Debt A	$0	$0	$0
Debt B	$4,000	$250	$250
Debt C	$3,000	$50	50+100+300=$450

OUR BIGGEST MOTIVATOR

Through this shoebox conversation, we discovered that together we were paying hundreds in interest charges to credit card companies each month. Like the congregant whose debt prevented him from working for his church, we found that we couldn't give to the causes or situations God put on our hearts. We wanted to give, but we were bound by another master.

We were paying hundreds in interest each month to these companies for purchases we had made years ago (and had since forgotten). As a result, we were able to give only about $10 to any need we saw. Which was incredibly frustrating because it was our God-given desire to impact the world through our giving.

We realized that if we paid off the credit cards, then we would instantly free up hundreds of dollars each month—which lit a fire under us. We then were able to simply transfer the hundreds we had been paying to Mastercard (who we didn't care about) to causes we deeply cared about and that had an eternal impact, without cutting into our personal spending at all.

This was a game changer.

Imagine life without debt. Imagine how many hundreds of extra dollars you would have available each month. What would you do with it? What would you do with an extra $300 each month? What about $500? $1,000?

This is an important question to ask because when you get a glimpse of what's on the other side of debt, it'll help you stay motivated through your financial journey.

My dream for you is that you'll be so free financially that when God leads you to start a business, go on a mission trip, give a significant amount, or anything else, you'll be ready and able to say yes!

CHAPTER 11

OUR THREE RULES FOR MASTERING CREDIT CARDS

redit cards are kind of like chain saws. A chain saw is a relatively dangerous power tool that hurts a fair number of people
each year. But when I need to chop up a big tree, I use it responsibly
and it provides a lot of benefit. Like most tools, I can use it for my
benefit or, if I'm not careful, my harm.

Would I loan my chain saw to just anyone, not knowing whether
that person could use it responsibly? Not at all. The same should be
said about credit cards.

Because of the potential of harm from credit cards, some tend to
think that credit cards are inherently evil, but they aren't any more
evil than mortgage companies, credit unions, or student loans.* They
are simply one of a variety of financial tools available to us today
that, if used, need to be used wisely.

Any tool you use, including a chain saw, should improve your life,
not harm you. If you can use a credit card to improve your financial
situation, then continue to use it wisely. If not, then lose it and use a
different tool.

Should you choose to use credit cards, then I recommend following our family's three rules to help you use them responsibly.

---

* From the readers who've shared their stories with me, I actually believe student loans
are a bigger threat to our generation's financial health than credit cards.

LINDA: I once heard Jess Connolly say, in reference to a particular habit that she had, that she wasn't leaving room for God to do a miracle. I think of credit cards without rules in the same way. Overspending has become a habit for many of us. When we need a little extra, we just charge it and we begin to put our trust in the credit card, rather than God! But what happens if we draw a line in the sand and decide to put some strict rules on our credit card use? Is it possible that when we limit ourselves, we see God's unlimited power at work in our finances?

OUR THREE RULES

We use a debit card for most of our day-to-day expenses. But we also responsibly use a credit card each month as well.

At this point we are 100% debt-free (including having paid off our mortgage), and my goal is to never pay a dime of interest for the rest of my life. These rules help ensure that I reach that goal while also getting some of the benefits credit cards offer.

1. Don't Use Them for Discretionary Expenses

The truth is you are likely to spend more with a credit card than you would if you were using cash. The trick to prevent this is by creating a system to ensure that you don't.

One way we do this is by never using credit cards for discretionary expenses. These would be things that tempt us to spend more than we should. In our household, these expenses include eating out, clothing (for Linda), Lowe's (for me), groceries, and household goods.

Instead, we use our credit card only for non-discretionary expenses, such as the internet bill, insurance payments, utility bills—you get the picture. When we use it this way, we maintain control of our spending because there isn't ever any temptation to spend more than we should.

Simple Insight

If you set up budget billing with your utility companies, you'll find that most non-discretionary expenses tend to be about the same each month. This makes it pretty easy to schedule an automatic payment from your bank to your credit card each month.

---

2. Never Carry a Balance

There's a rule among the self-defense crowd that the best way to win a fight is to avoid it at all costs. If using a credit card without carrying a balance is a struggle, then just run and avoid the fight altogether. Use a debit card. Take the credit card out of your wallet and hide it in a closet somewhere. If it's still a temptation, drop it in the shredder!

When Linda and I got married, this was us. We didn't have the first rule and couldn't control our spending. So we closed down all our credit cards. We paid for everything with either cash or debit cards. We lived without a credit card for seven years.

Once we had more solid financial footing—and matured a bit—we decided to try again. Before we opened an account, though, we made a pact: if we couldn't pay the balance in full, even one time, we would close it down. It was only after that agreement that we opened a great rewards credit card. Which leads me to the third rule.

3. Make Your Credit Card Work for You

Most people don't understand how much of a gaping divide there is between an average rewards program and a good one. It's not like two times better; it's more like 10 to 50 times better. It can be the difference between getting $50 in rewards and getting $1,600 in rewards after using your card all year.

From cash back to miles, the benefits with a good rewards card can be huge. The people who don't think there is much of a difference just aren't using the right cards. Additionally, the fraud protection most cards offer is a nice perk. Many companies also provide consumer purchase protection such as extended warranties and insurance.

So, if you're going to use a credit card, please don't use it just because someone gave you a free T-shirt to sign up. Do your homework and find a good one. When I look for a credit card, here are some points I consider:

- **Annual fee:** All things being equal, I would prefer no fee, but some provide such great rewards that a $99 annual fee might be worth it.

- **APR:** This is your interest rate. In general, lower is better, but if you follow our never-carry-a-balance rule, it'll never matter because you won't be carrying a balance. Additionally, some cards offer a lower intro APR (i.e., 0% for 12 months) for new purchases and occasionally for balance transfers as well.

- **Balance transfer fee:** This is how much you have to pay to transfer the balance from one card to another. Let's say you have a card with a $5,000 balance and a 24% APR. If you find another card that has a promotional offer of 0% on balance transfers for 12 months, then it might make sense to pay a 3% balance transfer fee ($5,000 x 3% = $150) to have a 0% interest rate for 12 months.

- **Earning rate:** This is the rate at which you earn rewards. One point per dollar spent is pretty common, though the value of points varies quite a bit.

- **Sign-up bonus:** Many cards offer huge bonuses (I've seen bonuses as high as 100,000 points). There are typically spending requirements (i.e., spend $2,000 on the card within three months) in order to get the bonus. We had an entire 10-day hotel stay covered by a single bonus, so there is a lot of potential here.

It's easy to get overwhelmed by all the options. There are a lot and they are always changing. If you want a head start, though, you can check out seedtime.com/cc to see what we are currently using and my most up-to-date recommendations.

A FEW OTHER POINTS WORTH MENTIONING

You Don't *Have* to Have One to Build Credit

While a credit card paid off each month is one way to build a credit history, it isn't the *only* way. You can build your credit by paying student loans, car loans, credit-builder loans, rent (if reported), and sometimes even utility bills.

You Don't Need One to Rent a Car

Many years ago, it was difficult to find a car rental company that would let you use a debit card, so you were stuck using a credit card. Luckily, that is no longer the case. Almost all the major car rental agencies will let you use a debit card.

You Don't Need One for Emergencies

I know that is a bold statement. But this is why many financial coaches (including me) recommend an emergency savings fund. It's so much more fun (well, it's never fun, but it is *more* fun) to pay for an emergency with cash than to go in debt for it.

Saving up a $500–$2,000 emergency fund is a great place to start. But remember, when an emergency strikes, don't run to your savings or a credit card. Instead, run to God, your real provider, and prayerfully see how He would have you handle it.

THE KICK-START

PART 1

A ll right. It's time to tuck your cloak into your belt like Elijah and take the natural steps so God can do the supernatural unhindered.

1. START TRACKING YOUR SPENDING

(Read pages 25–34 for a refresher.)

If you aren't already tracking, today let's find out exactly where you are spending your money. At the time of this writing, personal capital.com is the tool I recommend for this job, but feel free to check out seedtime.com/cashflow for my most up-to-date recommendation and a video tutorial of the process.

Or if you prefer, you can go the old-school route and write down every purchase you make. It will take a little longer, but either option will help you begin to see what's actually going on with your spending.

○ Pick a tool and start tracking your spending.

2. CALCULATE YOUR AUM

(Read pages 11–18 for a refresher.)

This challenge is all about calculating your Assets Under Management (AUM):

○ Use the instructions laid out in chapter 2, or download our free tracking sheet at seedtime.com/aum to calculate your AUM.

○ Set a reminder on your calendar (or ask Siri, Alexa, or Google to remind you) to update this every six months to see your progress.

3. MAKE SOMETHING AUTOMATIC

(Read pages 33–37 for a refresher.)

Use the space below to create a list of all the things you can automate. Here are some ideas to get the wheels turning:

○ Use your bank's bill-pay service to automatically send money for monthly bills or giving.

○ Schedule an automatic transfer to move money to a savings account every month.

○ Work with HR to contribute a portion of your paycheck to your retirement plan.

_____

_____

Now choose one item from your list and make it automatic. Automate just one thing. Eventually you can come back to this list and automate the rest. But for today, one small step forward *is* a victory.

4. GET HONEST ABOUT ACCOUNTABILITY

(Read pages 45–50 for a refresher.)

I want you to ask some tough questions: *Is my money management method (budget, spending plan) actually holding me accountable? What deterrent is there to prevent failure?*

If you have a budget or spending plan that is holding you accountable and helping you reach your financial goals, then just imagine that I'm giving you a high five and a free pass for this one. But if not, try setting up the One-Category Budget.*

The goal is to find an approach to managing your money that holds you accountable. Whatever system you use, it should make it hard to fail and easy to succeed.

- O   Determine whether what you're currently doing is holding you accountable.

- O   If not, set up the One-Category Budget to create some accountability for your spending.

5. FIND YOUR WHY

(Read pages 51–59 for a refresher.)

I've heard it said that "he who has a *why* to live for can bear almost any *how*."[1] It's no different with our financial lives. We need a big motivating reason for making financial changes. Today we daydream. Seriously. Set a 15-minute timer, and just dream about what the God of the universe could do in your financial life. Go big here.

---

*   To take it a step further, check out our Real Money Method training: seedtime.com/real.

After all, we serve a big God. If you're having trouble, here are a few questions to get you started:

- Why did you buy this book?

- What dream is your financial situation preventing you from moving toward?

- What change in your financial life are you wanting to see? What is at stake if it never changes?

○ Today, get clear on your why. Use the space below to write out your motivations.

_____

_____

_____

○ Extra credit: Go to seedtime.com/why to get a printable PDF that you can write your motivations on. Put it where you can see it every day—so that as we continue, you can remind yourself why you're doing this.

PART 2

EARN ALL YOU CAN

In the hands of [God's] children, [money] is food for the hungry, drink for the thirsty, raiment for the naked: it gives to the traveller and the stranger where to lay his head. By it we may supply the place of a husband to the widow, and of a father to the fatherless. We may be a defence for the oppressed, a means of health to the sick, of ease to them that are in pain; it may be as eyes to the blind, as feet to the lame; yea, a lifter up from the gates of death!

—JOHN WESLEY

When I was 22, I got an entry-level position deep inside the belly of a financial services corporate headquarters. Even though I was on the bottom, I set a goal to be in a corner office of this skyscraper within 10 years.

To me, a corner office was the quintessential corporate success symbol. It would be proof that I had made it in corporate America. Proof that I was significant. Proof that my work mattered. I was full of ambition but off to a slow start.

The company had applied Henry Ford's assembly-line model to my department. Everyone had a single task to do over and over and over and over again. Eight hours each day. And I hated every minute of it.

I initially thought, *I'll just work hard. I'm good at working hard. If I work hard enough, I'll get promoted to something better and can still reach my goal in 10 years.*

Over the next couple of months, I discovered a couple of key problems with my plan. First and most painful to admit, I wasn't actually good at my job. I was supposed to process the 40 to 50 applications that came in each day by entering all the data from the applications into the computer. Bored yet? I almost fell asleep just typing that sentence.

After about three applications, my mind would start to wander. *I wonder if I would get caught if I started playing* Snake *on my cell phone for a few minutes. I wish I could listen to the new Coldplay album right now, but I left the CD in the car. Focus, Bob! Get back to work—you have only 42 more applications to do, and then you can leave.* And so on and so on.

Picture, if you will, asking a three-year-old to sit still and not make any noise during church—for eight hours. That was me.

The second flaw in my plan was that my competition for the next promotion had been doing this job for 10 or 20 years. They knew how to handle all the unique scenarios that came up—and there were many. And like you would expect, the veterans were a lot faster. To top it all off, most of them didn't seem to suffer from shiny-object syndrome like I did.

So, if you were the boss, who would you promote? The relatively new kid, who is slow and constantly distracted, or the veteran, who knows all the answers and is focused and efficient? Pretty easy decision.

MY TURNING POINT

After another year of hard work and struggling, I finally landed a small promotion. That's when I realized my chances of landing a corner office were slim if I stayed in this department. If I wanted to advance my career, I would have to find my way into a department with more growth opportunities.

Thankfully, I was nearly finished with my bachelor's degree in business. I thought, *This will get their attention. As soon as I have this framed and embossed piece of paper that cost me $50,000, HR will be pushing high-paying job offers in my face left and right.*

Now that I was a college graduate, it was time for me to make some *real* money. I was feeling good! Strutting around like John Travolta from *Staying Alive,*[*] blessing a variety of hiring managers with the privilege of being given my résumé.

To my horror, no one seemed to care about my college degree. Every department I applied to was more interested in hands-on experience.

After applying internally for numerous positions with no success,

---

[*] Do yourself a favor and google "John Travolta strut" to see what I mean.

I finally landed a position in a new department. I watched Ivy League grads in their three-piece suits walk the halls in a setting that looked exciting, fun, and incredibly lucrative. This was it, the big time.

The starting pay wasn't much better than my previous job—it was basically a lateral move, which was pretty disheartening, but I tried to stay positive. After all, it looked like there was a lot more room for growth in this department, so I decided to stick with it.

I soon discovered that I wasn't really in the department that I had thought I was being hired for. We were on the same floor, but the social standing of and opportunities for each group were *very* different.

After a year or two, I became painfully aware that people on my side of the cubicle wall rarely advanced out of this department. Almost all my coworkers were lifers who had been there for many years or decades. I found myself pigeonholed into a position with very little room for advancement, much like the previous one— pretty much a dead-end career path with few transferrable skills. And to make matters worse, I found that I wasn't good at this job either.

I felt trapped.

But it was all about to change. One day the perfect job opening came up outside the cubicle walls. I immediately applied. It would be a huge pay raise—about a 40% increase—and would likely lead to other promotions. Surely this was the breakthrough that I had been praying for all these years.

I went through two successful interviews. I knew the hiring manager and had worked closely with him in the past. Plus, I had more college education than anyone else applying and more experience to boot. In my mind, I was the only applicant who made sense for the position. Every metric pointed to me. I was so confident that Linda and I were already planning on how we would spend the pay raise.

I still remember the exact time of day, the papers stacked on my desk, and even how many clouds were in the sky when I received the mass email from my boss congratulating a coworker of mine for getting the position.

It was the slow-motion gut punch that dropped me to my knees. I felt like I was stuck on a desert island and the only plane I had seen in years had just flown by.

I was devastated.

I viewed it as confirmation that I was doomed to a job I hated and mediocrity for the rest of my life. It felt like my prayers for a breakthrough, for God to intervene, were falling on deaf ears. I was doing everything right, and it seemed to make no difference.

I had considered leaving multiple times but always felt that God wanted me there and that I shouldn't leave. It made no sense at all. Another year went by, and with every passing month, I felt more forgotten and stuck. The dream of a corner office was a distant memory.

> LINDA: Herein lies the importance of believing in your spouse when he or she has lost all hope. So use your words to encourage, and remember to be a warrior in prayer. I remember moments when Bob was so discouraged that no amount of encouragement helped. But fighting in prayer for him during these times was the most helpful thing I could do.

I needed a respite from all the pain of my career failure. I longed for purpose with my work. So on a whim I started a blog to share what I was learning about money. And even though my mom and grandma were pretty much the only ones reading what I was writing, it gave me some sense of purpose in life.

GOD'S TURNING POINT

One fall day in 2007, my boss squeezed our whole department into the conference room for a meeting. Because of the recent merger, every one of us was going to be laid off. People were crying. Many of them had worked together for decades, and as trapped as I felt, I was still young and could start over. Many of the others would struggle to find another job in our city.

If I hadn't been so callous and beaten up, I probably would have been more freaked out by losing my income. But honestly, I felt like there wasn't much further down I could go.

I finally mustered the strength to begin looking for any job I could find just to pay the bills. But I felt unease in my heart, and I knew something wasn't right. After much prayer, I realized that the Lord didn't want me to look for another job. Instead, He had a different, crazy path for me to walk. God wanted me to work full time on my fledgling blog.

This was 2007, mind you. Most people didn't know what a blog was, even fewer read them, and there was very little money to be made blogging. I had been spending about 10 hours a week on my blog for the previous year and was making about $2 an hour from my time invested. To add to the stress, Linda had a very low-paying job *and* we were trying to pay off $46,000 of accumulated consumer debt. *Are You sure, God?*

I often wonder how Moses felt when he lifted his staff to part the Red Sea. Did he think, *Really, God? You want me to point a stick at the sea, and it's going to make a way for us to escape?* While I don't know how he felt, this was my Red Sea moment, and it felt just about as illogical to me.

But I decided long ago that either God is who He says He is or He is not. And either I am going all in with following God or I am out. There is no in between for me. It was time to tell Linda. I shared with her where I felt God was pulling me. I was sure she would think I was crazy. To my surprise and her credit, Linda felt like it was the right thing to do.

I wish I could say that every day I walked in bold faith with that John Travolta strut, confident that God was going to come through, but many days I struggled. What was going to happen next? How were we going to pay the rent and buy groceries?

My blog was barely earning enough to pay the electric bill, let alone replace my day job. I was terrified that I was going to fall on my face. I was scared of what everyone would think if I failed.

But as we chose to trust God, Linda and I stood in awe as we watched Him do miracle after miracle. In just nine short months, my blog was generating more income than my previous day job. Six months after that, my mind was blown when I realized our new blog business was now bringing in twice as much.

The increased income was just icing on the cake, though. For the first time in my life, I absolutely *loved* the work I was doing. The joy and satisfaction I received from doing work that I was gifted for and excited about had been so foreign to me. It was one of the greatest blessings I could have been given.

In turn, Linda and I were able to bless others. The extra income put us in a position to help one of our pastors buy a much-needed car. With God's blessings, many giving opportunities that we had only dreamed of before were now becoming possible. Chasing this dream that God had placed in my heart had paid off. And it was exceedingly and abundantly above and beyond all I could imagine.[1]

To this day, I'm so thankful that God didn't answer my prayer to get that promotion all those years ago. It looked like the best path at the time, but He had something so much better for me.

* * *

A year or two into running my own business, I decided it was time to move my office out of the home and rent some space. I found the perfect building. It was close enough to home that I could ride my bike, it overlooked a beautiful lake, and it had all the amenities that I would need and more.

Only one office unit was available to rent. When I met the agent in the parking lot to check it out, he informed me that, because of an ownership change, it was being offered for a 50% discount.

Wow, I thought. *This just keeps getting better and better.* He walked me down the hall, opened the door, and said, "Take a look around, and let me know what you think."

I stepped inside, and tears began to fill my eyes.

It was a corner office.

As I stood in that office that had represented success in the corporate world, it now represented something so different to me. It represented God's faithfulness and grace. I didn't even care about the corner office anymore. I was just overjoyed to be able to do work that I loved and that left me feeling fulfilled beyond measure.

God had taken my shaky faith and obedience and used them to fulfill a dream. As you pray about increasing your income-producing ability, it might not come easy, but stay strong and obey God and watch what He does. He is working even when you can't see that He is!

THE RIGHT MINDSET

With any formula, all the elements work together to get a certain result. Change the parts of the formula, and you'll get a different answer. The same goes for the formula in this book: save, earn, give, and enjoy. When the parts aren't performing their intended functions, the results will be radically different.

It's critical to understand the reason behind "earn all you can." We aren't chasing money for money's sake, but rather, we are earning all we can to maximize Kingdom impact. In my case, my desire for promotion was misaligned. I wanted a corner office to prove to others that I was important. If I'm honest, I wanted to make more money for a lot of the wrong reasons.

But when I focused on the real reason for making all I could and stopped chasing that corner office, God intervened.

LINDA: Man, I love this part of our story. It sounds like a movie! But I would hate for the meaning to get lost because it doesn't sound like something that happens to real people.

For as long as I've known Bob, he has wanted his own business. The plan had been for him to climb the corporate ladder first. But as I watched him struggle, I knew his natural gifts and talents didn't line up with where he was. I yearned to find a way to help him. But my ideas were way too small compared with what God had in mind.

Each one of us is called to use our gifts in different capacities.

It's such a beautiful thing to watch the giftings God placed inside each of us come out in ways that have an impact on our world and bring glory to Him. He is full of surprises, and you never quite know how He's going to do what only He can do.

YOUR UNIQUE CALL TO EARN

Earning all you can looks different for each of us in different phases of life. I know several pastors, stay-at-home moms, and even people in corporate America purposefully *not* earning as much as they could. They intentionally chose a lower-paying path because they were following God's direction for their lives.

But in the context of what God has called us to, we should ask ourselves, How can we steward our time and talents well? How can we "work heartily, as for the Lord" with everything we put our hands to?[2]

For someone in corporate America, it might mean climbing the corporate ladder. For a business owner, it might mean better serving clients, which leads to business growth. For a stay-at-home mom, it might mean something as simple as selling the kids' old toys on eBay during nap time.

The point is that some of us are called to more overt and traditional forms of ministry and some of us are called to more covert forms of ministry. But it is all ministry.

We all have the opportunity to be used by God each day. We are all parts of the same body working together for the same cause. How will you steward your time, talents, and money to help expand His Kingdom?

CHAPTER 12

MONEY IS A TERRIBLE MASTER
BUT A GREAT SERVANT

In May 1962, a coal mine fire started in a small town called Centralia, Pennsylvania. It spread to mine tunnels, and because of the high carbon monoxide levels, all the local mines closed. Numerous attempts were made to put the fire out, but the narrow tunnels in multiple directions made it difficult and dangerous to access. So the fire continued to grow.

> As the years went on, the ground beneath the city itself became hotter and hotter, reaching over 900 degrees Fahrenheit in some locations. Smoke poured from sinkholes and gas filled basements. Residents started to report health problems and homes began to tilt. "Even the dead cannot rest in peace," wrote Greg Walter for People in 1981. "Graves in the town's two cemeteries are believed to have dropped into the abyss of fire that rages below them." Earlier that year, a 12-year-old boy fell into a sudden sinkhole created by the fire, barely escaping death.[1]

Ultimately, officials decided that further attempts at extinguishing the fire would be futile and that the best course of action would be to buy out the residents and then condemn all the houses and other buildings, thus creating a ghost town.

Even today that coal mine fire still rages on hundreds of feet underground in Centralia. Experts expect it to continue for another hundred years.

By contrast, did you know that the average forest fire lasts only 37 days?[2] So, why is it that the coal mine fire can burn uncontrollably for so long? What has made it nearly impossible to stop? There are a couple of key factors:

1. **It's difficult to access.** Putting out any wildfire is a challenging task, but when you have access to the fire, it certainly helps. Coal mine fires that burn deep underground in narrow tunnels are very difficult to reach and extinguish.

2. **Nearly unlimited fuel.** Oftentimes the coal deposits in coal mines run deep and wide. This particular mine in Pennsylvania has seemingly endless deposits that will fuel the fire until all the coal is consumed.

LIKE FIRE, LIKE MONEY

Fire has been used as a tool for thousands of years. When it burns in a fireplace, it keeps us warm. On the wick of a candle, fire provides light. It can easily be controlled and used for good. But without the proper safety measures in place, it can cause tremendous amounts of harm.

Like fire, money is a dangerous tool. It can be used for good or to cause harm. And like fire, money isn't evil, or good, but is amoral. And as long as people have been using money, it has been used for both evil and good.

But when it's in our hearts, money becomes incredibly destructive, not only to us, but also to those around us. Just like the coal mine:

Our hearts are difficult to access. In fact, we don't even know what's in the depths of our hearts. Only God knows. Greed can hide in the shadows and is often difficult for us to notice, let alone extinguish.

Additionally, there is a never-ending amount of fuel. Proverbs says, "The eyes of man are never satisfied."[3] There is never a limit to how much we desire. As the story goes, when John D. Rockefeller, one of the richest men to have ever walked the earth, was asked how much is enough, he was said to have responded in a way that accurately reflects this truth: "Just a little bit more."[4]

Money becomes dangerous when it's not controlled and we let it settle into our hearts. As Jonathan Swift puts it, "A wise man should have money in his head, but not in his heart."[5] How do we keep money out of our hearts, though? How can we use it as a tool to glorify God and advance His Kingdom?

BREAK YOUR TRUST IN MONEY

When I was 13 years old, my parents sent me to summer camp. I remember being led up to a high platform while all my friends and other peers watched from below. Once I was in position, the camp leader instructed me to turn around, lean back, and fall.

As I stood there, I felt everything in my body telling me *not* to fall. For over 12 years, my body had both consciously and unconsciously worked to *not* fall every time I was on my feet. And now, here I was, trying to do the exact opposite. Confusion swept over my nerve endings as my mind attempted to change the protocol. And not only change it. I was asking my body to do something that completely defied its duty of self-preservation.

My mind understood the command to let go and fall, but my body was resisting. I knew they were going to catch me. I could rationalize that they probably did this day in and day out at this camp. I told myself, *There is no way they'd let me fall. They're going to catch me.*

But the only way I could show that I trusted my friends was to actually fall. I had to stop trusting in myself—my ability to keep myself standing—and trust them instead. To prove that my trust was in them, I had to simply let go.

So often we trust in our money to make our struggles disappear. But when we do, we put our faith in money, not our Provider. Biblical scholar John Piper says, "You can't trust in God and in money at the same time. Belief in one is unbelief in the other."[6] It's time to break our trust in money. And it really is just as simple as the trust fall at my camp: let go.

The best way I know to let go of my trust in money is by giving— it's an incredibly effective antidote.*

We see the remedy in Matthew in the story of the rich young ruler.[7] This rich kid had it all. He had followed all the laws but was bound by his love for and trust in money. The cure? Jesus prescribed generosity.

And in Luke, we have Zacchaeus, a wealthy chief tax collector Jesus visited.[8] He was despised for his greed. We don't know exactly what Jesus said to him, but we do know that after Jesus left, he gave half his wealth to the poor. It sure seems like, in order to break Zacchaeus's love of money, Jesus gave him a prescription similar to the one He gave to the rich young ruler.

In both of these instances, when Jesus encountered people who had placed their trust in money rather than God, He prescribed giving as the remedy.

LINDA: I've found consistent giving to be the best way to say no to our flesh and remind ourselves who is really Lord.

Let's be honest. It's simple but not easy. Whenever faced with giving in a way that feels uncomfortable, I return to that trust fall all those years ago. I'm a 13-year-old boy again, experiencing that same resistance to letting go, that same desire for self-preservation.

But falling six feet and landing like a feather in my friends' gentle hands was unlike anything I've ever experienced. At first, I felt out of

---

* This is why the third part of the formula (coming up soon) is so crucial.

control and helpless. I was clinging only to the hope that they would come through for me. And when they did, it was exhilarating. I wanted to get back in line and do it again.

You know what? Every time God has led me to give in a way that goes against my innate desire for self-preservation, He has always come through too. And every time, I experience that same exhilarating thrill as I land like a feather in God's gentle hands. Just like after that trust fall, I find myself eagerly waiting for the opportunity to do it again.

MAKE MONEY THE SERVANT

I don't think many of us choose to make money our master, but when I take an honest look at past decisions I've made around work and earning a living, far too often my decisions have been based solely on the financial implications.

Should I accept this job offer? I should have prayed to find my answer; instead, I often just considered whether the new job paid more than my current one. That certainly sounds like money (rather than God) was the master, doesn't it?

As you know, our society has become obsessed with chasing money. The world tells us to hustle and grind and do whatever it takes to get more money. And somewhere along the line, we bought into the lie that money is the goal, when what God intended all along was that it would simply be a tool to help us fulfill our purposes on earth.

> Somewhere along the line, we bought into the lie that money is the goal.

Author Craig Hill explains that when "money is [the people's] servant . . . they do what they do to fulfill a calling given to them by God. Since God is the master, money becomes their servant, to fulfill God's purpose and calling on their lives."[9]

Chasing money just to fulfill our own self-focused desires is a recipe for trouble. Instead, the mandate should be to maximize earnings for God's purposes. For whatever He wants us to do with the increase.

HOW MUCH YOU EARN IS NOT THE ISSUE

I often get the question, "Is making a lot of money wrong?" My answer is always the same: The amount of money someone earns isn't the issue. What matters is the heart.

Someone who lies and cheats to get ahead doesn't automatically become honorable once she has more. On the other hand, a generous person who earns more doesn't automatically become stingy and greedy.

Money simply reveals and amplifies what is already within the heart of a person.

Author Mike Michalowicz puts it like this:

Money amplifies your character. It is that simple.

It allows you to repeat your ingrained habits easily. And unless you have developed a strong, humble character coupled with good habits, more and more money will become more and more of a problem.

For example, if you have a drug addiction (a bad habit) and you get tons of money you are likely to do more drugs. Money amplifies the bad habit. It amplifies the character.

What about Mother Teresa? What happened when she got tons of money? She used it to serve more orphanages. She used it to do more of her good habits. Here too, money amplifies character. . . .

It has no judgement. It just enables you to be more of you.[10]

FUEL FOR THE JOURNEY

In the rest of part 2, I'm going to give you a lot of fuel to propel you forward financially. The last thing I want is to fuel an uncontrollable coal mine fire in your heart. But I do want to help you get all the fire-wood you'll ever need to keep your family warm and have plenty to share with others for God's glory.

While I don't know your heart, God does and can help us get our hearts in the right place. So let's prepare for the journey ahead. Join me for a moment to pray before we go any further.

> *God, like David, I ask that You would search me and know my heart and point out anything in me that offends You and that You would create in me a pure heart.[11]*
>
> *I choose to affirm that You are the Lord and Master of my life and that money will be a servant to fulfill Your purposes and calling in my life.*
>
> *May my trust always be in You, regardless of how much or little money I have in my bank account. When times are lean and when there is an abundance, help me always be aware that You are the Provider of all my needs.[12]*
>
> *May I be content with, thankful for, and aware of the blessings You've provided me. I pray that, like Paul, I would be able to learn the secret of being content in any situation.[13]*
>
> *I pray that You would provide an abundance for every good work, and I ask for wisdom to steward what You have entrusted me with.[14]*
>
> *In Jesus's name,*
> *Amen.*

CHAPTER 13

FOUR KEYS TO EARNING MORE
IN THE DIGITAL ERA

"How many times a week do you have sex?"

I turned to Linda and asked, "Do we really have to answer this?"

We did. Along with many other super personal questions for a whole bunch of strangers to read. Sitting at our kitchen table at 9:45 p.m., staring at a huge stack of papers, I decided I was done answering questions for the night.

We were in the process of adopting our first child. It's a humbling process that requires you to let go of a lot. Unlike having a baby the old-fashioned way, you actually have to pass a long series of tests to ensure that you are deemed worthy of raising a child.

> LINDA: And we have no regrets; adopting is one of the most beautiful things we've been part of! Every awkward question, tedious form, and evaluation was nothing compared with how thankful we are for our child.

As we waded through the piles of paper, I discovered that we had to hire not one but two highly specialized adoption attorneys (one in each state). At the time, each attorney charged no less than $400 an hour.

What? I thought. *Now I have to give up control of my finances too?* There was no way of knowing how many hours they would work, so

I wouldn't have control of how much I paid them. But I had no other option. I had to pay the attorney fees. After the shock and anxiety came curiosity: *Why is it that they can charge $400 an hour and people will pay it?*

In my last corporate job, I made $17 an hour. Asking my boss to give me a $2-an-hour raise would have been a stretch. So, what was the difference?

While there were certainly a variety of factors at play, the biggest difference was that our lawyers were indispensable and I wasn't.

LINDA: Turns out, adoption lawyers are indispensable because they are highly specialized. There is so much to know about protecting children, and the laws differ from state to state. And international adoption has its own laws based on the country and its standards as well.

In general, your earnings as an employee, freelancer, or business owner are directly proportional to how indispensable you, your services, or your products are. If you want to earn more, your products, services, or you need to become more indispensable.

This is why you will never find a *legit* high-paying job with no experience required. It's basic supply and demand. There are millions of people with no experience, so there is no need for the employer to pay high dollar to fill that position. On the other hand, there are very few highly specialized adoption attorneys (only a handful in our entire state), and when you have to have one, you pay a premium.

My curiosity about the $400-an-hour lawyers led me to begin investigating common threads of those who get paid well versus those who don't. As I dug in, I found four common traits among those earning a significant income:

- They operate within their passion and calling.
- They keep learning and honing their craft.

- They solve a significant problem or make something better.

- They operate where demand is high.

Now, other factors that are out of our control are always at play, but some of the best career advice I've received is to focus on what I can control and ignore the rest.

So, while there are always exceptions, in most cases high-income earners share many or all of these traits. The more of these traits you have, the better your chances of becoming indispensable and, as a result, earning a significant income.

THE KEYS IN ACTION

My brother-in-law, Tom Bills, is a luthier. That means he builds guitars, but not just any guitars. He builds super high-end custom guitars that cost more than most people pay for a car. He's one of the best in the world at what he does, and he's been doing it for over 20 years.

He's had the first two keys taken care of for a long time. He's insanely passionate about building great guitars, and over his career he has sought out master luthiers and learned from them as he continued to refine his craft.

Even though his guitars sell for over $25,000 apiece, he can build only a handful of them every year. The profit margins are relatively small, which can make it tough to make a living. Adding to that, the high-end guitar market is a fickle one that shifts with the economic cycles. The demand for these types of guitars can change seemingly overnight.

A few years ago, however, Tom discovered a demand for something he had overlooked, something that worked with his gifts and his passions. For years he'd been getting emails from beginner guitar makers, all asking him for tips. It dawned on him that he could probably supplement his income by creating an online course sharing what he has learned.

Now he's teaching new luthiers how to build guitars, sharing his strategies with students all over the world. His training has exploded in popularity, quickly becoming his most significant source of income. As we look at Tom's story in light of the four keys, we see that he checks all the boxes:

- He operated within his passion.

- He invested in his education and skills.

- He created a better and more convenient way for luthiers to learn guitar making.

- He looked for where demand was the greatest.

So, what if you don't have any of these with your current work? That's okay. You don't need to be perfect at all four of them, but the more of these keys you have working together, the better. And you'll be on a path to becoming indispensable and increasing your earning potential in this decade and beyond.

TWO PATHS TO AN EXTRAORDINARY CAREER

Scott Adams, famed creator of the *Dilbert* comics, says there are two paths to being extraordinary:

1. Become the best at one specific thing.

2. Become very good (the top 25%) at two or more things.

Adams argues that the first one is incredibly difficult. Think making it to the NBA, writing a Grammy-nominated song, or creating an app that gets bought by Google. In my relatively short career, almost all my failures were a result of me trying to be the best at something where the odds were incredibly slim.

But the second strategy is a lot more accessible. As Adams explains,

Everyone has at least a few areas in which they could be in the top 25% with some effort. In my case, I can draw better than most people, but I'm hardly an artist. And I'm not any funnier than the average standup comedian who never makes it big, but I'm funnier than most people. The magic is that few people can draw well and write jokes. It's the combination of the two that makes what I do so rare. And when you add in my business background, suddenly I had a topic that few cartoonists could hope to understand without living it.[1]

Later in my career when I transitioned into blogging, I found a unique combination of skills. I didn't know everything about money, but I did know more than most. I wasn't the best writer, but I was better than the average Joe. I wasn't the best marketer, but I had an aptitude for it. Even though I wasn't in the top 1% at any of these skills, that combination of three "pretty goods" provided a competitive advantage that helped me earn a healthy full-time living. And that allowed us to eat and live indoors—which made Linda happy. Right, honey?

LINDA: I love *not* camping. I'm what you call "indoorsy."

So, if you can't be the best at one specific thing, then seek to become very good at two or more things that set you apart.

CHAPTER 12

CALLING AND PASSION:
FISH DON'T CLIMB TREES

Let this sink in: you are fearfully and wonderfully made. You are God's masterpiece.[1] You aren't a second-rate creation compared with your brother, mom, Instagram friends, Elon Musk, or anyone else who seems to have it all together.

God created you *exactly* the way He wanted—and for a critically important purpose. We have each been given unique abilities to serve Him and make an impact on the world. God doesn't make mistakes. Let me say that again. God doesn't make mistakes.

But the world has tricked us into playing a comparison game. Inside the game are hierarchies and ways to quantify our self-worth and value in society. We assign positions in this system based on SAT scores, grades, job titles, net worth, and dozens of other man-made metrics. Sadly, many of us draw conclusions about our own worth and the worth of others from these lies.

With all the amazing complexities of human beings created in the image of God, why would we ever base our worth (or someone else's) on a few man-made metrics? There's a quote that's commonly attributed to Albert Einstein that always comes to my mind when I consider the breadth of our individual gifts: "Everyone is a genius. But if you judge a fish by its ability to climb a tree, it will live its whole life believing that it is stupid."[2]

As someone who has many times felt like a fish trying to climb a tree, that quote is particularly meaningful to me. I have spent a lot of time working at jobs I wasn't gifted for. Jobs where I could work as hard as I wanted but it didn't really matter because someone else better suited thrived while I struggled. It felt like running into a strong headwind; I was working my tail off and had few results to show for it.

For many years I was trapped in the lie that God hadn't created me with the same intentionality as others. I'll never forget how liberating it felt when I found my calling. This fish quit trying to climb a tree, discovered a pond, and began to swim.

Steve Jobs, looking back on how he got fired from Apple, the company he had created years prior, said this: "I'm convinced that the only thing that kept me going was that I loved what I did. You've got to find what you love. . . . The only way to do great work is to love what you do. If you haven't found it yet, keep looking."[3]

If you are a fish, I hope you have found your pond. If you are a tiger, I hope you have found your jungle. If you are a bird, I hope you have found the air. But if you haven't found your place, don't stop seeking. When you find it, your life will never be the same. And the world needs you to be doing what you were created to do.

There's a famous scene in *Chariots of Fire* where Eric Liddell, a runner who plans to be a missionary, decides to put the mission field on hold while he trains for the Olympics. As Liddell defends his choice, he says, "When I run, I feel His pleasure. To give it up would be to hold Him in contempt. . . . It's not just fun; to win is to honor Him."[4]

No matter whether others understand or agree, operating in the giftings God placed in us brings Him pleasure. It benefits us, honors God, and positions us to make the biggest impact on the rest of the world.

I imagine most of the greatest advancements in our world have come through people who loved their work and were using their God-given gifts to the fullest. Let's be honest, they probably didn't come from people who hated their work and were just trying to get through the day.

LINDA: I believe God created us with such intentionality that if we only knew, we'd be facedown in worship until we go to heaven. And not just the things we deem to be beautiful either. The "flaws" are intentional too. They're all there to bring Him glory.

Years ago, I received clear direction from the Lord about a situation I felt led to help with. When I shared what was on my heart with someone whose opinion I valued, she said, "Oh, you're just a rescuer, and that's why you feel that way."

I felt dismissed and labeled, and I struggled to figure out whether she was right. Thankfully, a wise pastor counseled me and said, "So what if you are a rescuer? What if God put that in you to do this very job? What if this is the perfect attribute to help in this situation and it was intentional? What if God created you that way on purpose?"

> What if the thing someone told you to stop doing is actually the most important part of who God made you to be?

I never saw it the same way again. Every attribute I have, I now see as God's design. And every character trait (when under submission to God) is exactly what He intended. It's in me for a reason, no matter what others think or say about it. God put it there, so I'm going to seek Him for how to use it.

So, I want to ask you the same thing. What if the thing someone told you to stop doing is actually the most important part of who God made you to be?

When we are fully who God created us to be, He gets the glory because we can do the things He has put on our hearts, and that, my dear friend, is the whole reason you are here: to bring God glory.

RUN TOWARD YOUR CALLING

Sometimes it's hard to pinpoint your calling, and other times it's like an old friend that's been with you for years. If you know what you're passionate about, run *toward* your calling. Don't run away assuming you can't make money with it. Whether it's organic gardening, knitting, analyzing numbers, getting to know people, shopping for clothes, or really *anything else you can name*, there's probably someone making a comfortable living from that same passion.

That doesn't mean it's going to be easy. There may not be a well-worn path directing you where to go, and the climb may get rocky. But it's worth the chase. Don't concede to spending your whole life doing work you're *not* passionate about—there is more for you!

And if you don't know what you're gifted to do, then take heart, my friend. Everyone's journey to this discovery is different. Here are a few questions that might help:

- What comes easier to you than to most?

- What feels like work to others but feels like fun to you?

- What can you do that leaves you wondering why most people aren't good at it?

For many of us, it's hard to see the forest for the trees. We're often too close to our gifts or passion and can't seem to see them amid the day-to-day tasks. In these moments I often suggest asking an honest and direct friend or spouse for his or her opinion. What does that person think you're passionate about? This is often a good clue.

Another great way to unearth your passion is to look at your journey so far. A seasoned gardener can look at seedlings and get a clue of what kind of fruit the plant will produce. Even a novice gardener can deduce the difference between carrot, tomato, cabbage, and squash plants long before the harvest. So it is with our lives.

In his book *The Art of Work,* Jeff Goins explains, "A calling is what you have when you look back at your life and make sense of what it's been trying to teach you all along."[5]

When you consider the unique circumstances you've faced, the obstacles you've overcome, the types of things you've been drawn to, you'll often see a pattern. These are the clues that God has given you.

YEAH, BUT . . .

Once we identify our giftings, it can be hard to move forward. There are an endless number of "yeah, but" scenarios:

- You live in a small town, and the possibility of pursuing your passion is limited.

- You might feel like you missed your time. Now you're too old and it's too late.

- You feel like you don't have time to devote to the process.

- [Insert hundreds of other reasons you may feel stuck.]

I get it. I've felt the same way. Perhaps your story is similar to mine. I was passed over, forgotten about, looked down on, and a no-body in the eyes of people whose approval I was trying to win.

I was working hard, but I was getting nowhere. My professional life was a growing string of failures, and my hopes were dashed.

Jeff Goins accurately describes this season of my life:

Every calling is marked by a season of insignificance, a period when nothing seems to make sense. This is a time of wandering in the wilderness, when you feel alone and misunderstood. To the outsider, such a time looks like failure, as if you are grasping at air or simply wasting time. But the reality is this is the most important experience a person can have if they make the most of it.[6]

THE PATH FORWARD

How can we make the most of a dark period in life? How can we find a path forward?

If you're where I was, then try to focus on these four things to make the most of this season.

1. Work Heartily for the Lord, Not People

When you hate your job, the tendency can be to slack off and do the bare minimum. It can feel like it doesn't matter what you do because no one will notice or care. The truth was that my boss might not have noticed or cared but God did. He was using this to see whether I passed the Colossians 3:23 test: "Whatever you do, work heartily, as for the Lord and not for men."[7]

On the other hand, maybe you're stuck in a job where you don't have the luxury of slacking off but you're hating every minute of it. Your bigger challenge may be maintaining a healthy attitude during this challenging season. People often assume that *heartily* only means "to work hard." But I've come to realize that it means so much more. It's working hard with a cheerful heart, knowing that your work is glorifying God, even when you can't see that it is.

Whether I had a good or bad boss, was paid poorly or well, or loved or hated my job, I was called to work diligently and with a joyful attitude—not for my boss but for God. When I fully grasped that idea, it brought peace. I knew that even if I had a tyrannical boss, things would work out for me if I worked for the Lord. I didn't have to get caught up in brownnosing or jumping through hundreds of hoops to keep the boss in a good mood. I just needed to work hard and trust God to take care of the rest.

2. Pray and Cling to Hope

We have the assurance that God will work things out for the good of those who love Him.[8] Even when it seems impossible and every fiber of your being wants to give up, cling to hope. And when discouragement creeps in, battle it with the Word and prayer.

During this challenging period of my life, I would get to work early, sit in my car, and spend 20 to 30 minutes praying and reading the Bible before I went to battle for the day.* This is how we fight our battles, right? I laid my troubles at God's feet and prayed for grace and strength to stick it out.

3. Maintain a Thankful Heart

It's easy to dwell on the negative. It's easy to talk about how bad your job, boss, or coworkers are. But does that ever really help? During my dark season, I found help in 1 Thessalonians 5:18: "Give thanks in all circumstances; for this is God's will for you in Christ Jesus." I took this verse to heart and began to thank God on a daily basis. *God, thank You that I'm not standing in the unemployment line. God, thanks for my car to get to work. God, thanks for keeping my car from being broken into.* I would seriously look for anything I could be thankful for. And it changed my entire attitude.

Maintaining a thankful heart and choosing to see the positive in very negative circumstances is incredibly challenging, but I'm convinced that this was one of the primary reasons I was able to stick it out.

---

* The passage that I often found myself meditating on was Psalm 37. It's a powerful chapter that sustained me on some of my weakest days.

4. Actively Try New Things

The boy with five loaves and two fish probably couldn't have imagined what Jesus could do with them.[9] But he took what he had and let Jesus do His thing.

It was during this season in my life that I decided to start a blog. It was mostly just something to take my mind off my trials. I had no idea what could come of it, but I started blogging anyway. Had I not been putting some action to my faith by starting a blog,[10] I would probably still be in a job that I hated.

I don't know what being active means for you. Maybe it's starting a business on the side; maybe it's studying to prepare yourself for where you want to go with your career; maybe it's taking classes to make yourself a more valuable asset to an employer. But whatever it is, continue to put action to your faith.

Your Kick-Start

Want to jump ahead and complete your related challenge? Go to page 154 for details.

If you're struggling to find your passion and feel trapped in life, remember that God wants to be involved. Looking back, I see His hand in my situation and His glory on full display. If you let Him, He will be active in your story as well. He wants to work through your dark season and show you just how magnificent He is. But we must show up.

This isn't easy. In fact, it's incredibly difficult just to keep showing up. But it's one of the most important decisions you can ever make.

Be intentional in your first step on this incredible journey—believe God can do it.

I'll leave you with another thought from Jeff Goins: "Sometimes all it takes to make a difficult decision is an affirming voice telling you what you know to be true but still need to hear."[11]

Let me be that affirming voice for you today. God is bigger than your circumstances. Your life is far more significant than you realize. And He isn't finished with you yet. Let's go.

LINDA: Let me check in with you if you have a spouse who is going through something like this. Don't stop encouraging. One of my absolute favorite things about being married is being able to see things in Bob that he's blind to. It's in these moments that I get to remind Bob who God created him to be.

Your spouse, best friend, parent, or sibling may be in this type of situation. You can counter the lie in his head that says, "You're not good enough. There's no way out. This will never end." Keep telling him who he is—not who life has beaten him into but who God created him to be.

Pray; speak Scripture over him; encourage him! And lovingly cheer him up every time you see him succumb to discouragement. You have the power to change things!

CHAPTER 15

EDUCATION: KEEP LEARNING AND HONING YOUR CRAFT

In 2010, Tyler Blevins was in college and working at a fast-food restaurant. Eight years later, he was making almost a million dollars—per month—playing a video game.[1]

Most of us had parents trying to prevent us from playing too many video games. Growing up, maybe you heard something like, "No one will ever earn money playing video games. You're wasting brain cells, time, and my money by having that TV on for three hours straight."

Yet here we are. Professional gamers exist, and like Blevins, some of them make millions playing games. This didn't happen by accident. Like anyone else who is truly great at something, the world's best gamers have a natural gift *and* have put in the hard work. They spend countless hours honing their craft. But why would they choose to dedicate years to learning and practicing? Because they *love* it.

If you're anything like me, you might not have enjoyed school. You might not associate learning with fun. But the reality is this: most of us like to learn—if it's about things we're actually interested in.

I might not have loved traditional school, but I loved learning how to throw a curveball and strike somebody out. And I love learning songs on the guitar (even if I have to struggle with a song for weeks). And even after all these years, I love learning more about money because I'm passionate about it.

The great thing about the 21st century is that almost every skill has some sort of income-earning opportunity associated with it.

There has never been a time with more opportunity to earn by doing whatever it is you love.

But you have to put in the work.

The point is this: find a craft you love; then educate yourself and develop your skills. You'll find that education and practice are essential keys to success that will never become obsolete.

OPERATE WITHIN YOUR CONTROL

Many things that are out of our control affect our ability to earn money: the economy, competitors, Google's algorithm, office politics, and more. With so many big factors outside our spheres of influence, it can be easy to get discouraged. But remember, control the things you can and forget about the things you can't. In other words, operate within your control.

We can control our ability to learn and develop our crafts by always looking for ways to grow. While you don't have control over the natural giftings you were given, every human being has the ability to improve herself. And indispensable people actively look for ways to add value by improving themselves. For ways to become better at what they do—just a little bit each day. Thankfully, it has never been easier to learn.

If you're stuck in the mindset that learning is limited to traditional education, then let me be the bearer of good news: we live in the digital age. From audiobooks, ebooks, to YouTube to podcasts to online courses and, yes, even traditional college, there are an endless number of ways—some with a price tag and some completely free—to learn about an endless number of topics.

MY PROCESS FOR LEARNING SOMETHING NEW

You might be thinking, *Okay, Bob. I hear you. Education is essential to becoming indispensable, and there are a million ways to learn. How do I start, though?* Well, it might vary wildly depending on the topic, but over the years, I've developed a simple (and kind of obvious) approach to learning about most topics. Let me walk you through it with an example. Imagine you want to learn how to bake sourdough bread. Here are four simple steps you could take.

1. Search Google and YouTube

Start by searching Google and/or YouTube—"how to bake sourdough bread." Next, read or watch 5 to 10 results that you find. Simple, right? There's more. Some of these results will likely be junk, and some will be good, but what you're looking for at this point are the common threads—the basic principles and building blocks to begin structuring your understanding.

Assuming you knew nothing about the topic, this will almost certainly give you a massive leap in understanding. And most importantly, it will allow you to build a mental framework so you can fill in the details as you continue to learn and practice. It won't make you an immediate pro at baking sourdough bread, but in very little time, it will make you considerably better than you were yesterday.

2. Practice, Practice, Practice

While reading, listening, and watching others is an important part of the learning process, it doesn't mean anything until you start applying what you've learned. In this case, try to bake your first loaf of sourdough using what you learned in step one.

As you attempt to bake that first loaf, you're likely to make mistakes, which will yield more questions. And when questions arise, seek out those answers. Oftentimes it will involve revisiting step one but refining your search on Google or YouTube to find that specific answer. In the case of sourdough bread, it might be searches like "how often should you feed sourdough starter" or "how to work with sticky dough." As you find these answers, your understanding of the subject will continue to expand.

3. Find the Most Authoritative Books on the Subject

Books are a wealth of information where most writers store their best stuff. In addition, the ideas are often clearer and explained better than in a video or blog post. While it's not always the case (think video game techniques, for example), I've found it to be true for most topics.

It can be tricky to find great books on certain topics, so I like turning to Amazon or Goodreads. You can quickly see what cream has risen to the top. If those avenues fail, try googling "best books on [subject]" and look for what books are mentioned repeatedly. Soon you'll find three to five of the top books on the subject. As you read (or listen) to these books, you'll continue to fill in gaps in your knowledge.

4. Master the Skill (or Not)

According to bestselling author Malcolm Gladwell, becoming a master of any given topic takes roughly 10,000 hours.[2] Can you imagine dedicating every minute of your life for just over a year to one skill? That's a lot of bread.

Most of us don't need to reach this level of baking, so mastery would be overkill, and it makes more sense just to have a working knowledge.

You won't go through all four steps with every skill you seek to learn. There are many microskills that I will never pursue to mastery, but I've gotten great value from them by using the first three steps. For example, as I've been on this book-writing journey, I've sought to learn how to find an agent, how to write a book proposal, how to best outline chapters, and many other writing-related topics. I don't need to be the best in the world at writing a book proposal, but having a working understanding of how to create a great proposal has been quite helpful.

There are only two topics that I'm even attempting to go to step four with: the Bible and money. They are the topics that are most valuable to me in my field of expertise and that I've chosen to devote my life to. For each, I've read hundreds of books and thousands of articles, sought out mentors, and practiced what I learned for years. I'm not sure where I am on that 10,000-hour path to mastery of these subjects, but I don't really care. I just keep learning about each because I love learning about them. I can't get enough. And when you find what you love, it's easy to crave learning.

THE VALUE OF MICROSKILLS

Remember, you can use the first three steps to learn a skill without spending 10,000 hours to master it. I like to call these microskills, and there are likely hundreds that could benefit you in your work or career.

For example, let's say Jennie is a real estate agent. Some microskills that could help her become a better agent might include learning how to:

- communicate and listen better

- negotiate more effectively

- market herself as an agent

- increase her knowledge of related businesses (i.e., mortgages, underwriting, credit scores, inspections, etc.)

- become better at researching

- network more effectively

- remember names better

- obtain more leads on houses

- manage time better

- use email marketing to engage with clients

- become a notary

If you look around, you'll likely find that most people aren't improving themselves with microskills. And this, my friend, is how you can stand out from the crowd. While Jennie won't need to go past step two (practice) for most of these, if she were to improve herself with even half of these microskills, then you can bet she would be a highly sought-after agent.

Your Kick-Start

Want to jump ahead and complete your related challenge? Go to page 155 for details.

I love how Proverbs 22:29 puts it: "If you are uniquely gifted in your work, you will rise and be promoted. You won't be held back—you'll stand before kings!"[3]

Of course, developing all these microskills won't happen overnight. Learning is an investment that takes time. But when you realize that learning produces knowledge and understanding that you can carry with you for the rest of your life, it's easy to get excited about it.

The goal is to continually improve, to make growth a habit. Over time you'll begin to see your efforts paying dividends in the form of more impact and more income. As you do, continue learning and never stop making the most of the gifts God has given you.

CHAPTER 16

SOLVE A PROBLEM OR
MAKE SOMETHING BETTER

In the 15th century, one of the undisputed greatest innovations of all time emerged. Johannes Gutenberg took the printing press technology that had been around for many hundreds of years and made it better.

Prior to his improvement, most books were copied by hand, while some were hand cut into wood, stone, or metal, then transferred to paper. It was time consuming and costly, which left books in the hands of only the wealthiest families.[1]

The Gutenberg press could print far faster than previous printing methods and at a much cheaper cost to the printer. His invention allowed for the mass production of books and furthered the spread of knowledge to all people, not just the ones who could afford it.

Because of this, his innovation literally changed the history of the world. Everyone, not just priests, now had access to the Bible, which fanned the flames of the Protestant Reformation. The Gutenberg press also launched a global news network, kicked the Renaissance into high gear, enhanced the accuracy and spread of scientific studies and data, and more.[2]

If you study history, you'll find that most of the greatest inventions didn't just come out of left field. Many were improvements on previous ideas or techniques. Even Isaac Newton wrote in 1675, "If I have seen further, it is by standing on the shoulders of giants."[3]

But innovation isn't reserved for inventors and scientists. We have the same opportunity to make an impact on the world through our work. We just need to look for problems to solve.

SOLVE MORE PROBLEMS

A surefire way to increase your income is to solve more problems or simply make something better. Look around at the products, apps, or services you buy or hire out for. Odds are you're paying to solve problems.

Simply put, business is getting paid to solve problems for people. Whether you're the owner, CEO, or middle manager or you're in the mailroom, you have to solve problems for your customers or boss. The bigger and better the solution, the more vital you become, and better compensation usually follows.

We paid our adoption attorneys $400 an hour to solve a unique problem for us. Meanwhile, a Chipotle employee might be making $12 an hour. The Chipotle employee gets paid less because making me tacos is a much easier problem to solve. The bigger the problem, the more you can charge.

Regardless of whether you are a freelancer, business owner, or employee, you have the opportunity to solve more problems or make something better. These won't all be Elon Musk–level challenges, like working to eliminate fossil fuels or building a colony on Mars. But there is a never-ending list of problems available for most of us to solve.

If you're an employee, a simple recipe for success is to reduce your boss's problems. As bestselling author Tony Robbins says, "The secret to wealth is simple: Find a way to do more for others than anyone else does. Become more valuable. Do more. Give more. Be more. Serve more."[4] Let's start today looking for problems that we can solve for our clients, customers, or bosses.

THE 11-STAR EXPERIENCE

A great way to generate some innovative ideas is to brainstorm what an absurdly amazing experience would look like for your boss, customers, or clients. I like using the 11-star experience exercise from Brian Chesky, the cofounder and CEO of Airbnb.[5]

This is how it works:

1. Write what a 1-star experience would be for your customers, clients, or boss.

2. Write what a 5-star experience would be.

3. Continue describing 6-, 7-, 8-, 9-, 10-, and 11-star experiences (far past the point of being realistic).

Business coach Bryan Harris took Chesky's exercise and laid out an example of what this might look like using Airbnb:

- **1-star:** I go to the website and it takes forever to load. I sit there for 2+ minutes and leave out of frustration.

- **3-star:** The website loads! But when I search for a place, only a few results come up. One looks OK. I message the host with a question but still haven't heard back 2 days later. I'm annoyed, but book anyway.

- **5-star:** I find multiple incredible places. The hosts respond to questions within minutes. When I show up to the place I book, the host greets me with a smile. It's spotless, has an amazing view, and the host is easy to reach whenever I need something.

- **7-star:** Gift bags are waiting for my wife and me when we arrive. Our names are on them. Cheese . . . and chocolate truffles are arranged throughout the place. We're blown away.

- **9-star:** After booking, the host sends a care package to our house. A car is waiting for us at the airport when we arrive at our destination. We enter the house and find a personal chef making dinner. After dinner, a masseuse is waiting for us.

- **11-star:** Elon Musk picks us up from the airport. We ride on the back of an elephant from the airport to the house. A giant parade of people welcome us. Elon flies us on a private trip around the moon.[6]

You might be asking yourself, *Why take it to the extreme, Bob? There's no way I could offer an 11-star experience—that's laughable.* You're right. But by taking it to the extreme, you'll uncover ideas from the 6-, 7-, and 8-star experiences that might just be within your reach.

Chesky explains, "The point of the process is that maybe 9, 10, 11 are not feasible. But if you go through the crazy exercise, there's some sweet spot between 'They showed up and they opened the door' and 'I went to space.' That's the sweet spot. You have to almost design the extreme to come backwards."[7]

What I love about this exercise is that it generates ideas to make something better or to solve an unseen problem. If you're struggling to come up with things you can improve on or problems to solve, definitely try this out.

A TREE DOESN'T PRODUCE FRUIT OVERNIGHT

If you do one act of 7-star service for your boss or a customer and then go back to consistent 3- to 4-star service, it probably isn't going to yield much fruit. But if you consistently go above and beyond, you will get noticed. And most importantly, it will be honoring to and noticed by God—who, after all, is the true source of our promotions.[8]

Regardless of whether you're a business owner, freelancer, employee, volunteer, or stay-at-home parent, you're most likely serving others. How can you blow their minds by going above and beyond what is expected? How can you go beyond a 5-star experience for those you serve?

Your Kick-Start

Want to jump ahead and complete your related challenge? Go to page 156 for details.

I'll leave you with this timeless wisdom often attributed to Napoleon Hill: "The man who does more than he is paid for will soon be paid for more than he does."

LINDA: I want to give a shout-out to all the stay-at-home parents out there and chat with you a little about this. This 11-star experience can apply to you as well!

I've been a stay-at-home mom for seven years now, and let me tell you, I honor you. You're doing a great job. You are *such* a valuable asset to your family. No one else does what you do, and even though it can seem unnoticed, I see you! I see your hard work and I applaud you!

When you have a newborn, it's an all-you-can-do-to-survive season. And for good reason. It kicks your butt! However, when I started moving out of that season, I think I was in a recovery mode that lasted longer than it should have because I started to spoil myself.

Some days I needed a nap, but some days I didn't. Yet I would still "nap when they napped" because I just felt like it. Instead, I could have used my time more wisely to help the family. If you're in that season and your family is needing extra income, I have two options for you to consider:

1. Take on a side hustle to bring in more money.
2. Serve your spouse well so he or she can bring in more money.

Bob and I pretty much share the household duties. He is actually the chef in our house (yeah, I know!), and he really does like it! Most of the time. But when he's working extra, I can either be annoyed that he's not making me food or I can 11-star this bad boy and figure out how to help.

I may not make a gourmet meal (seriously, he's such a good cook; I wish we could have you over for dinner!), but I can make some basic things that get food in our bellies. I may not update our investment portfolio (I'm honestly not even sure what that means), but I can update our budget. I may not use the Weedwacker, but I can mow the lawn (or make our eight-year-old do it). Get my drift?

When I make any effort to help him out, he is so grateful! Because when he feels like he's drowning, he appreciates a life raft even if I can't pull him out of the water.

I think it's a good idea for us to ask ourselves, *What can I do to contribute?* Even if you're not currently working, you might be able to help bring in more income, whether directly or indirectly.

CHAPTER 17

DEMAND: GIVE THEM
WHAT THEY WANT

In 1853, a young man saw people heading out to California during the gold rush, each one trying to strike it rich by panning for gold. Instead of being like 99% of miners who ended up going back home broke, this entrepreneurial 24-year-old decided he was going to look for where demand was greatest.

After hearing that the miners desperately needed more durable work pants, young Levi Strauss decided to meet the demand. Well over 100 years later, his blue-jean company is still going strong and has generated far more income for him and his family than even the luckiest gold miners of his day got from mining.[1]

> Our work isn't about us. It's about serving people.

Our work isn't about us. It's about serving people. It's about preferring them over us. Giving them what *they* demand.

Fast-forward about 150 years and you'll find Amazon. It is changing how the world shops because it has focused on what customers want much more than its competitors have.

- Customers wanted to be able to buy the best product out of the 10 listed. Amazon listened and let customers review products *on its website.* This was an incredibly bold move at the time.

- It broke from the status quo of laborious online checkout and made the checkout process as fast and easy as possible.

- It constantly pushed the envelope on quick deliveries— because, of course, everyone wants it faster.

Amazon made decisions based on what its customers wanted instead of the systems it had in place. Amazon put its customers' desires first. And we all got to watch this little online bookstore become the behemoth we know today.

So, if you run a business or are a freelancer, this might make sense. But what if you are an employee? As an employee, you can still ask yourself, *Who are the people I serve each day?* You may have regular customers, or you may have employees or volunteers that you manage. Even if you aren't talking to actual customers, you are serving your boss and are likely interacting with coworkers. Think of these individuals as your customers. How can you serve them better today?

> **LINDA:** Years ago, Bob mentioned how his thinking changed about being an employee after he became an employer. "I just need someone to fix these problems," he'd say. He told me that if he were looking for a job now, he would try to make the boss's life easier. Because making the boss's life easier is great job security.

HOW DO I KNOW WHAT MY CUSTOMERS WANT?

1. They Might Already Be Telling You (or at Least Hinting at It)

Even if you aren't asking your customers, coworkers, or clients what they want from you, some of them might just be bold enough to tell you. I've heard it said that if your customers or audience ever asks for something three times, make a product to meet that demand.

A videographer from my church became known for the unique effects that she used in her videos. She would often receive calls and emails from people asking her to share the video effects. She, almost reluctantly, began selling them on the side and quickly found herself with a business generating far more revenue per hour than her primary business.

The farmer I buy many of my veggies from each week at the farmers market reasonably assumed that most people at the market just want to buy their veggies. But he was constantly being asked what variety of tomatoes he grew and where to get the plants. So he listened to his customers and began selling veggie plants at his stall. The plants have become a huge part of his business and contributed to his biggest revenue year to date.

Do you have a boss who is dropping some hints or flat-out telling you what he would like from you? Freelancers, are your customers or clients regularly asking you whether you know someone who does _____? Do you have the skills and time available to offer that service? If it's within your ability, then consider taking steps to offer it.

2. Ask Them

We all love sharing our opinions, right? So lean into that, and ask your customers what they want. But the key is to make it as easy as possible for them. Every tiny amount of friction reduces the number of responses you'll get.

Simple Insight

You can use Google Forms to create a quick and dirty survey for free. Or surveymonkey.com for more bells and whistles.

Business owners: Send an email asking your customers what their biggest wants, needs, and challenges are. Ask how you can help. Or send an email saying you are considering rolling out one of four new products next quarter and asking which would interest them most.

Your Kick-Start
Want to jump ahead and complete your related challenge? Go to page 156 for details.

Employees: Talk to your boss. Tell her you are wanting to develop yourself and become more of an asset to her or the company (this right here will score a lot of points). Ask her for suggestions on things you could grow in to make yourself more valuable.

Freelancers: Are there services you don't provide that clients keep asking for? What if you could realistically offer them those services? How would you do it? Send an email to your top clients, and ask them about their biggest problems and how you could help.

3. Listen to the Complaints

Oftentimes when people are complaining, they are just communicating what they wanted that they didn't get. This is a huge opportunity that is often overlooked. Those seemingly frustrating words can speak volumes on how to adjust to meet consumers' desires, and we need only listen.

Business owners: Read competitor reviews—particularly bad reviews of bigger competitors. This is gold. Look at the common complaints people have. Keep an eye out for patterns.

This will often lead to some clear direction on what customers want and can spark plenty of great ideas.

Employees: Listen to what your boss or coworkers are complaining about. "Man, Bob is always three minutes late. It drives me up the wall." Clearly this means they value punctuality. So, what if instead of arriving exactly on time—as expected—you decided to get to your desk 10 minutes early every day? To a person who values punctuality, that speaks volumes.

Freelancers: What are the things that freelancers in your industry are notorious for? How can you be the opposite?

4. I'll Just Tell You—They Want It Faster

This is a desire of pretty much everyone, and it's never going away. It has been an obvious obsession for Amazon that continues to this day. They understand our inherent human desire to always want things quicker. And they have been relentlessly innovating to get packages in our hands faster. As a result, I now scoff at the idea of having to wait four or five days for my package, which was the expectation 10 to 15 years ago.

Now most Amazon customers in metro areas expect delivery in one or two days. And over the years to come, we'll see that expectation drop to hours as Amazon continues to find ways to get us our stuff faster.

How can you structure your work or business in a way that gets your boss or customers what they want faster? While this isn't likely an easy problem to solve, as we have seen with Amazon, quicker services can really set you apart and make you indispensable.

CHAPTER 18

QUIT LIVING AS IF THE PURPOSE OF LIFE IS TO ARRIVE SAFELY AT DEATH

So, remember my layoff I've been telling you about? Well, even though this blog of mine was barely earning enough money to pay the electric bill each month, God had made it clear that it was to be my focus.

And I was cool with that. For a week or two. But as the bills started piling up, I realized we were going to burn through our savings very quickly if I didn't start bringing in more money fast.

Then it happened. An entrepreneur from church, who I really looked up to, offered me a job out of the blue. This wasn't just any job. It was work I was good at, work I loved, with someone I admired. On top of all that, it would pay twice as much as the job I had just been laid off from.

It was a miracle. My breakthrough had come. God had come through, and we were reaping the fruit of our obedience. I was so excited I never even thought to pray about it—I just said yes. *When can I start? I can start tomorrow. Or why not now? Let's start now!*

But God had something to say. While I didn't hear an audible voice, if God and I had been having a conversation, it would have gone something like this:

> **God:** *Nope. That's not it.*
> **Me:** *(turns up the music louder to try not to hear)*

> *God:* *That's not it.*
> *Me:* *Is that you, Satan? 'Cause clearly this is God's blessing. I prayed, we obeyed, and everything about this is perfect. It must be God's idea.*
> *God:* *Nope. God here. And no, that's not it.*

This was insane. Giving up a salary two times more than any job I had ever had in my life was crazy, right?

> *God:* *Keep following the vision I gave you. I have something better.*
> *Me:* *But, God, this is plenty good. I'm content with this. You tell us to be content in Your Word. Well, here I am being content. Let's just do this instead. Sound good?*
> *God:* *Can you trust Me? You'll be glad you did.*
> *Me:* *I can, but we need money, and this job would provide that.*
> *God:* *I can provide far better than any job. Trust Me.*

And with that, I grudgingly called my almost-boss back and told him that I regretfully couldn't take the position. Making that phone call was one of the most difficult things I've ever done in my life.

I had believed that having a source of income should always be my top priority, but God was trying to teach me that obeying Him is always the best move. He was asking me to step out and join Him on the crashing waves.

THE INVITATION

One day, a long time ago, a group of men piled into a boat to cross the Sea of Galilee. Jesus, who stayed behind, would meet up with them later. But the wind became so strong that the disciples were struggling to make any progress across the sea. Then, through the wind and the waves, they saw a figure walking toward them. Jesus was coming to meet them. He called to Peter, inviting him to step out onto the roaring sea.[1]

The disciples' boat—no matter how well built—could have been brought down by a bad storm. Boats can sink and can fail us. But Jesus never will. Walking on the waves with Him is safer than being anywhere else. And while it may not be easy, it's always worth the risk.

Over the years, God has met Linda and me in the storm. He has asked us to join Him on the waves. As we worked to pay down our credit card debt, He invited us to give *more* instead of less. Miraculously, we reached our goal years faster than anticipated. When we wanted to begin growing our family, He invited us to adopt, something I had never even considered. This road led to our biggest blessing yet—children so perfectly fit for our family.

When I was laid off, God invited me to start a business instead of looking for another job. His plans led to my greatest career success. And then a few years later, He invited me to take a yearlong sabbatical (as in no work for an entire year). I didn't know how I was going to be able to feed my family, but God provided all year long.

In each of these situations, it looked as if stepping out of the boat was going to make our lives worse and take us in the opposite direction of our goals. But every time Jesus invited us to step out to walk on the water with Him, He came through. Every. Single. Time. And it always yielded bigger blessings than we were expecting.

If I'm honest, I spent way too many years playing it safe and striving to avoid risk at all costs. But I decided I want to spend the rest of my days walking on the water every time Jesus invites me.

How about you?

LINDA: When Bob tells the story of getting laid off, I often get asked what I thought during this time. It was definitely a season of growth for us. We had the gift of time to make this decision, though. It allowed us to talk, think things through, and pray for a few months before making a commitment.

I was nervous, but the way Bob responded gave me confidence. The biggest reassurance he gave me was that if we needed money, then he wouldn't stop searching for a job until he found one. Even though he was looking for something above minimum wage, he assured me there was no job beneath him. He would work anywhere until he got a better job or until the blog started making money.

We had a timeline. If the blog wasn't making X dollars in three months, Bob would get another job. We also had a small buffer because he had received a severance package that would help for a few months.

But the biggest relief was that we were in this together. We were a team, and we were both on board with the decision. If I would have said, "Nope. Get a job, and we'll work on it on the side," he would have done it immediately. I really believe that the two of us working together on this is what caused the breakthrough. And I'm so glad we obeyed the leading of the Lord! Our lives have been so blessed because of it.

STEP OUT OF THE BOAT

Jesus tells us that He came to give us "life . . . to the full."[2] I love how Eugene Peterson puts it in *The Message*: "more and better life than they ever dreamed of." You want to know how to tap into this rich life that Jesus is inviting us into?

Say no to your comfort zone. It's the only way to fully experience what God has for you.

Far too many have laid down their dreams in exchange for comfort and the illusion of safety. It seems too risky to start that business that God put on your heart or to give how He is leading you or to break that habit you know you should. Friend, our comfort zone will

> Our comfort zone will always appear to be safer. But it's a lie.

always appear to be safer. But it's a lie.

When God is leading you, there is no safer path. In *Chase the Lion*, pastor and bestselling author Mark Batterson writes, "In every dream journey there comes a moment when you have to quit living as if the purpose of life is to arrive safely at death. You have to go after a dream that is destined to fail without divine intervention."[3]

If God has given you a vision, get after it. Leave the comfort of the boat. Take that leap of faith. Let Jesus show you the view from the waves.

> LINDA: The grace of God extends through everything that feels uncomfortable as long as you're following Him. We have grace all the time, and when we have to walk through something difficult because He asked us to, He never leaves us there. Stay tethered to Him, and you'll be amazed at what happens!

BRAVE THE WAVES

Taking risks is scary. Even when I choose to trust that God will deliver, I tend to be more like Peter on his first attempt to meet Jesus. I sink into the fear. What if it doesn't pay off? What if it fails? And it might. But what if it doesn't? What if Jesus lifts me out of the water and places my feet on the waves?

About 10 years ago, I bought two stocks. I invested $1,000 in each. Within three years, one of them was worthless and I lost my entire $1,000 investment.* Losing $1,000 is never fun and I wasn't excited

---

* Losing 100% of your investment in a stock is pretty rare, but it can happen.

about it. But the other stock I bought was Amazon, which went up by 1,500% in just over 10 years.*

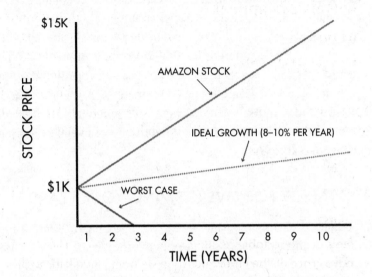

Both were unlikely scenarios. Here's the key, though: each stock had a downside potential of $1,000—the amount of money I invested. I would never lose more than $1,000. The upside potential, however, was unlimited.

Now, I say this not to share a lesson in investing† but rather to illustrate how often we aren't evaluating downside and upside potential accurately.

I find most people have a good idea of what the worst-case scenario would be. It's easy to focus on what we could lose. Where we struggle is imagining the upside potential. It's the unlimited that we're clueless about. I certainly was. I was so determined to settle for a job that was *better* but not God's best.

---

* Just so we're clear, this is also a rare situation when it comes to stocks.

† If you do want investing lessons, you can visit seedtime.com/investing.

Take an honest look at the actual risk of your endeavor. It's probably similar to those stock investments I made. It could go nowhere, and you could have nothing to show for it. Or God could intervene. Now, what would happen if you did go after it?

As Mark Batterson says, "You are one idea, one risk, one decision away from a totally different life. Of course, it'll probably be the toughest decision you ever make, the scariest risk you ever take. But if your dream doesn't scare you, it's too small."[4]

When God is in the equation, the upside potential is unlimited. So, what fear is holding you back? What risk do you need to analyze to put your fear to rest?

A STRATEGY FOR OVERCOMING YOUR FEARS

Whether it's starting a business, quitting a job, moving across the country, or anything else, it's important to properly analyze the situation as part of the decision-making process. But in order to analyze the risk, we need to face our fears.

Fear tends to distort our thinking and beliefs. It can cause us to overestimate the negative consequences, underestimate the upside potential, or ignore the cost of not taking action.

Just like monsters to a child, our fears loom large in the shadows. By shining a light on our fears, revealing them for what they are, we are able to face them, evaluate the risk, and make a plan to move forward.

I have found podcaster and author Tim Ferriss's fear-setting exercise to be very helpful in illuminating my fears.[5] When I need to evaluate the risk, this tool not only helps me accurately estimate the downside and upside potential but also highlights the cost of doing nothing. It often is the kick in the butt I need to move forward with God's plan for me.

THE FEAR-SETTING EXERCISE

Step One

Grab a sheet of paper, and divide it into three columns: define, prevent, repair.

Define	Prevent	Repair
1.	1.	1.
2.	2.	2.

In the first column, describe in vivid detail the worst-case scenario if you were to take action and move forward in your situation. Write out other terrible outcomes you can imagine. Be specific. Leave no fear, no nightmare, no what-if unturned as you imagine the change you want to make.

As Ferriss says, "Would it be the end of your life? What would be the permanent impact, if any, on a scale of 1–10? Are these things really permanent? How likely do you think it is that they would actually happen?"[6]

In the middle column, write out things you could do to prevent those scenarios from happening. What realistic actions could you take?

In the final column, write down the steps you could take to repair things if one of those scenarios did happen. If X happened, what could you do to make things better, even if not 100%?

Step Two

Grab another sheet of paper and label it "Potential Benefits."

Potential Benefits
1.
2.
3.
4.
5.
6.
7.

List all the potential benefits of succeeding or only partially succeeding. Think on all levels—not just financial. What are the implications for your family, marriage, spiritual life, and emotional health? Rate the impact of these benefits on a scale of 1 (no impact whatsoever) to 10 (unimaginably good).

Step Three

On the same sheet of paper (or another if you're out of space), create three columns: six months, one year, three years.

Cost of Inaction		
6 Months	1 Year	3 Years

In each column, describe what you imagine would happen if you did nothing. Be detailed. What are the consequences of not taking action in six months? One year? Three years?

Ferriss's questions drive home the urgency of this step:

What is it costing you—financially, emotionally, and physically—to postpone action? . . . If you don't pursue those things that excite you, where will you be in one year, five years, and ten years? How will you feel having allowed circumstance to impose itself upon you and having allowed ten more years of your finite life to pass doing what you know will not fulfill you?[7]

Oftentimes we default to inaction because it seems to be the most painless option, but that is rarely true. This exercise will reveal the true cost of not taking action.

MY FEARS LAID OUT

When I was considering going full time with my blog, I was paralyzed by fear because of all the risks involved. Here's how I walked through this exercise:

Becoming a Full-Time Blogger		
Define	Prevent	Repair
Blog never earns more than $100/month	Bring in extra income on the side—eBay biz? Work at Starbucks?	Find another job at a competing firm
All my severance and emergency funds dry up	Live off our survival budget for a year	Use job-placement assistance—can use up to a year after my end date

Potential Benefits

1. Please God by obeying His leading

2. Do work that feels meaningful to me (and get paid!)

3. Me = boss = freedom to set my own schedule

4. More time to spend with family

5. Higher income potential

6. Develop valuable skills

7. No cubicle ocean!

Cost of Inaction		
6 Months	1 Year	3 Years
Emergency savings would be depleted	Emergency savings completely gone, behind on rent payments by a month or two	Broke, evicted, living at Mom and Dad's
Not working on blog = less traffic = less income	Not working on blog = no traffic = no income	Blog dead and would have to start over from scratch
Disappointed in myself		

Once I saw my fears laid out, my perspective completely changed. Was I still worried about moving forward? Sure. This exercise didn't erase every speck of worry. But it did shine a light on my concerns and revealed that the potential benefits outweighed the risks.

I'll end this section with this advice from Tim Ferriss:

What are you putting off out of fear? Usually, what we most fear doing is what we most need to do. . . . Define the worst case, ac-

cept it, and do it. I'll repeat something you might consider tattooing on your forehead: What we fear doing most is usually what we most need to do.[8]

KEEP YOUR EYES ON GOD

At the end of the day, following God requires taking risks, and walking with God isn't some flowery bed of ease. He will likely call you to do scary things. But as scary as they might seem, He never leaves your side. And when God calls you, following Him is always the safest option.

Your Kick-Start

Want to jump ahead and complete your related challenge? Go to page 157 for details.

Frame your financial walk in the lens of obedience to God. Even when—especially when—it doesn't make sense. Choose to follow God rather than security, money, comfort, or anything else.

Follow God, friend.

THE KICK-START

PART 2

6. GET CLARITY ON YOUR CALLING

(Read pages 116–24 for a refresher.)

One of the best ways to begin getting clarity on what God has called you to do is by identifying your gifts.

Sometimes it can be difficult to identify our unique gifts and talents. If that's you, here are some questions that should provide some clues as to your gifts.

○ Take 15 minutes to answer these questions:

- What comes easier to you than to most?

- What feels like work to others but feels like fun to you?

- What can you do that leaves you wondering why most people aren't good at it?

If you're feeling stuck, ask your spouse, close friends, siblings, and/or parents to answer these questions with you in mind. What do they think you're gifted at or passionate about?

○ As you begin to identify those gifts, ask God how He wants you to use them.

○ If you're rock solid on your gifts and calling, then you get the day off.

7. IDENTIFY MICROSKILLS TO IMPROVE ON

(Read pages 125–30 for a refresher.)

If you want to stand out, focus on learning microskills to add value to those you serve.

○ Spend a few minutes thinking about 5 to 10 skills related to your profession. Write them below:

_____

_____

_____

_____

_____

○ Pick one off the list above, and commit to growing in it.

○ Schedule time in your calendar or planner to learn this skill. Look for videos or articles, and watch or read them. Start a to-read list for any books on the subject. Follow any masters of the skill on social media.

8. PROBLEM SOLVING WITH THE 11-STAR EXPERIENCE

(Read pages 131–36 for a refresher.)

The goal of this challenge is to identify overlooked ways you can better serve your clients, customers, or boss. And if you're a stay-at-home parent, remember that you still serve others. As you go through this exercise, think along these lines: How can you blow the minds of those you serve?

- ○ Grab a sheet of paper (or your computer), and spend 15 to 30 minutes completing the 11-star experience exercise.

- ○ What ideas can you pull from this exercise that you can implement (and maintain)? What can you begin today? What parts will take time to start? Make a plan to develop these new ideas.

9. IDENTIFY THE DEMAND

(Read pages 137–41 for a refresher.)

When you can identify what the people you serve want, you'll be on your way to becoming indispensable. The first step is often the simplest: ask them.

Employees: Make time to meet with your boss. Tell her you want to develop yourself and become more of an asset to her or the company (this right here will score a lot of points). Ask her for suggestions on things you could grow in to make yourself more valuable.

Business owners: Send your customers an email, and ask what their biggest wants, needs, and challenges are and how you can help.

Freelancers: Send your top clients an email, and ask what problems they are dealing with and how you could help. Try to turn this into a conversation to get deeper insights.

Stay-at-home parents: If married, talk to your spouse and brainstorm ways that you can help the household unit, even if you aren't actually earning.

○ Using inspiration from above or ideas of your own, take a step toward identifying how you can better serve your boss, customers, clients, or family.

10. FEAR-SETTING

(Read pages 142–53 for a refresher.)

Advancing in our professions seems to force us to face our fears, doesn't it? So it's time to get comfortable with them. This exercise will help you confront your worries and doubts, shine a spotlight on them, and call them out for the little devils that they are.

Even if you don't have any big fears holding you back, let's take this opportunity to identify the smaller ones that are almost always lurking in the shadows. Here are some questions to get you thinking:

- What has God led you to do that you have yet to take action on?

- What are some things you consistently procrastinate on doing?

- What triggers anxiety in your work life?

○ Complete the fear-setting exercise. (Check out seedtime.com/fearsetting to print off the PDF worksheet.)

GIVE ALL YOU CAN

Any temporal possession can be turned into everlasting wealth. Whatever is given to Christ is immediately touched with immortality.

—A. W. TOZER

E very year in the heat of the summer, Linda and I take the kids to the county fair. It has all the distinct elements you would expect: the smell of funnel cakes, the towering Ferris wheel, and the excitement on each kid's face. And as with many fairs, you can't use cash to go on any rides. You have to buy tickets. That is the de facto currency of the Williamson County Fair.

Every time, I find myself trying to make sure I use up all the tickets we bought. Why? Because the minute the fair shuts down, those tickets are worthless. Even if I had 1,000 tickets and could go on as many rides as I wanted, the minute the fair ends, they can't be used for anything at all.

Our lives on earth are like being at a fair. We can accumulate tickets in the form of bank balances, investments, and possessions, but when this show's over at the end of our earthly days, our fair tickets are worthless.

Well, except for when they aren't.

What if you had 1,000 tickets at the fair and every time you gave one to another fairgoer that person got to go on a ride and $10 was deposited in your bank account?

You'd probably spend your time at the fair giving away as many tickets as possible, right? Remember, they will be worthless in just a few days, but you have a small window of opportunity to exchange them for real currency that lasts beyond the fair. And that exchange is made simply by giving.

Can you see the smiles of the young families enjoying the rides they wouldn't have been able to afford? I can hear the laughter. I can see kids waving wildly as they pass by their parents on the merry-go-round. Creating such joy in the lives of others would probably make that day one you'd never forget. Then, after creating such joy, you would walk away with real currency that you could use for years to come.

This idea of converting fair tickets to real currency by giving them away isn't that far-fetched from how God connects our earthly giving and eternal treasure. Jesus Himself said, "Go and sell what you have and give to those in need; you will be making deposits in your account in heaven, an account that will never be taken from you. Your gifts will become a secure and unfailing treasure, deposited in heaven forever."[1]

Or as I might translate it, "Go and give away your fair tickets; you will be making deposits in your account in heaven, where you can build wealth that will last forever."

ALL THE MONEY I MADE WITH NETFLIX STOCK

Years ago, when I first signed up for Netflix, I thought about buying some stock. I liked the service, and it seemed to me that it might just be the future of entertainment. The price per share at the time was about $3. As I write this, each of those $3 shares is worth $488.

Want to know how many shares I bought?

Zero.

I didn't buy a single share.

Warren Buffett says, "The stock market is a no-called-strike game. You don't have to swing at everything—you can wait for your pitch."[2] But it's hard to look back at that Netflix-sized pitch, see how well it's done, and know that I didn't swing. In the same way, I don't want to get to heaven and be kicking myself for *not* storing up more eternal wealth when I had the chance.

In his book *The Treasure Principle*, Randy Alcorn says, "I'm convinced that the greatest deterrent to giving is this: the illusion that . . . Earth is our home."[3]

It's with this in mind that we step into part 3 of the formula: give

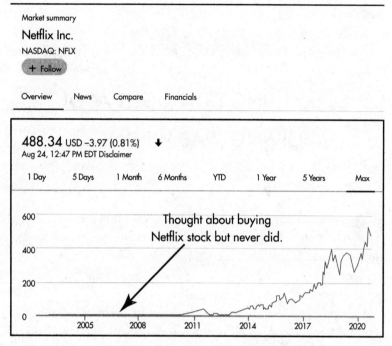

Market summary

Netflix Inc.

NASDAQ: NFLX

+ Follow

Overview   News   Compare   Financials

488.34 USD −3.97 (0.81%)   ↓
Aug 24, 12:47 PM EDT Disclaimer

1 Day   5 Days   1 Month   6 Months   YTD   1 Year   5 Years   Max

Thought about buying
Netflix stock but never did.

Source: "Netflix Inc.," Google Finance, www.google.com/finance/quote/NFLX:NASDAQ.

all you can. When we truly see our short stay on earth as the opportunity to store up "deposits in [our] account in heaven,"[4] it only makes sense that we would give all we can to fill up that account.

Not only do we benefit those around us and live lives of adventure and blessing; we also get to make deposits in our heavenly accounts. Not a bad deal at all. So let's use our fair tickets wisely. What do you say?

CHAPTER 19

EVERYTHING I THOUGHT ABOUT
GIVING WAS WRONG

One Sunday morning, many years ago, I sat in the pews of my small church waiting for a guest preacher to share his message. Bill, as I'll call him, had worked closely with Mr. Big Name Preacher (whose name I don't remember) and was about to speak. I could sense the excitement in the room.

The entirety of our 75-person congregation seemed eager to hear what Bill had to say. After all, it had to be really good if he had worked with Mr. Big Name Preacher.

I don't remember much of the message—I think it was on giving—but I do remember the scowl on his face. In fact, I don't recall him smiling a single time while he was behind the pulpit. At one point during his message, he angrily said, "Who here isn't tithing?"

My jaw dropped. Surely this was a rhetorical question, but the inflection in his voice indicated that it wasn't. He actually wanted an answer, and he wasn't going to move on until he got one.

What is happening right now? I thought. I had never experienced anything like this. I didn't have a job at the time, so I felt "safe" from his interrogation. Yet I noticed my palms beginning to sweat. I desperately wished I could crawl under my seat and hide.

The silence was deafening.

Bill just stood there and waited. I kept trying to think of ways to escape the painfully awkward moment. *Should I leave out the side door? Can I make it without him noticing?* But, with his audacity, only God knew what he would say to me as I walked out.

So I stayed. And it got worse.

Most times when I had seen preachers ask a question and not get a response, they moved on fairly quickly. But not this guy. He was as determined as an FBI agent, and he seemed to think it was his righteous duty to find the answer.

He reworded his question. And again. And a couple more times. The awkward moment stretched on and on.

Finally, relief came. Well, relief for me but not for the two guys who raised their hands to admit that they hadn't been *consistently* tithing. I know this because, believe it or not, Bill had a conversation with them about the specifics of their giving. From the pulpit. In front of us all.

I wish I were making this story up. But I'm not. We got to be 73 flies on the wall in this impromptu public "counseling session."

He then proceeded to call these two men up to the altar to repent before us all. We watched them walk up with their heads down like the saddest Charlie Brown you've ever seen. It was excruciating.

You might think that he would have let up a little at this point and shown some compassion. But he didn't. Bill continued to publicly berate them for "the error of their ways." The rest of us breathed a sigh of selfish relief—he wasn't after us anymore. Even though we all felt terrible for the two scapegoats.

At last, it ended. Both guys pitifully made their way back to their seats, and Bill continued with his message like nothing had even happened.

I was a new Christian at the time, and this moment shaped my view of giving. Since I didn't know much of the Bible, that was all I had to go off. It was a far cry from what I had hoped giving would be like. If this was what Jesus meant when He said, "It is more blessed to give than to receive,"[1] I didn't believe Him.

NOT IN RESPONSE TO PRESSURE

Hopefully, you haven't ever experienced anything like that. But I'll bet you have felt some sense of obligation or guilt when giving or even thinking about giving. It happens to me even at the grocery store.

I'll be standing in line with three other customers behind me; then the cashier asks something like "Would you like to donate a dollar for animal voting rights?"

Can I be honest with you? I hate when cashiers ask me this.

It's not that I think animals shouldn't have the right to vote. Or wait—do I? And it's not even that I don't want to give to support the cause. It's that I feel pressured. I feel put on the spot. I fear I'll be judged by these strangers in line behind me, especially if the two customers before me both gave.

I don't know any of these people around me from Adam (or Eve). Their opinions on whether I give or not shouldn't matter. Yet I let them pressure me into giving to something that isn't on my heart. They probably don't even know they are causing this stress.

For the longest time, I thought that the *only* reason people gave was in response to pressure, reluctantly and grudgingly. In church, maybe some of us give only because we know we should. We give reluctantly because we know how far that extra cash would go on the next Target run or how many date nights we could have with it. Giving feels like loss.

Sometimes giving is distorted by a well-executed marketing strategy that plays on our emotions. We give to certain charities because we feel guilty for the blessings we have and fear being perceived as greedy if we don't donate. Even Christmas gifts to our friends and family are ripe with guilt and quid pro quo: she got me something last year, so I need to be sure to get her something this year.

From what I could tell from Bill's message, giving was supposed to be a form of self-flagellation. Sort of like the ancient religious practice of whipping oneself as a sign of devotion. It was meant to be painful. It was marked by feelings of perpetual guilt, because even if I gave everything away and lived like a pauper, it wasn't enough to satisfy God.

Nope, giving definitely did not sound fun. There was no joy or other positive emotions in it because that would defeat the whole purpose of giving. I was convinced that guilt and obligation were acceptable motivations for giving, especially in the offering bucket.

Turns out, I could not have been more wrong. But before I could see the truth, I had to discover the root of almost all pressure-filled giving: guilt and shame.

THE DANGER OF GUILT AND SHAME

Most people would assume that greed is what the devil uses to curb generosity in our hearts, but I'm convinced that guilt and shame can be even more effective tools of the Enemy. Remember the story of the county fair? Remember the 1,000 tickets and the unrestrained thrill of giving them away?

I imagine myself in that situation, trying to figure out how to best use the 1,000 tickets. I see myself walking past the popcorn vendor when I hear murmurs in the crowd: "Bob is so selfish. Did you know that he plans to use some of those tickets for his family?"

I brush it off and try not to be fazed by it. But I hear someone else criticizing how I use my tickets. The judgments roll in, and I begin to question myself. *Am I giving enough? Should I be letting my kids use any of these tickets to enjoy the fair?* And then another calls out from across the crowd: "Bob, how dare you call yourself a Christian! If you were really a Christian, you wouldn't let your kids ride the three-ticket rides when some kids can afford only one-ticket rides."

With that, shame begins to fill my heart. The laughter of the kids is now nothing more than a shrill sound filling my heart with resentment.

The guilt and shame from those comments would suck any joy out of giving. Giving would become a miserable experience—really a punishment of sorts. I imagine myself meandering the fairgrounds, heavyhearted as I feel like I *should* give away these tickets. But with so much emotional baggage tied up in it, I can't bring myself to do it. I feel guilty. I shut down. I give up.

Over the years, I've talked with countless readers in the SeedTime community about giving. I've found that when people feel pressured by shame or guilt, they don't give more. They give less. And they despise it.

But here's the thing: this is not God's plan for giving. We're not supposed to give based on guilt or shame. Instead, God has a better path: "Decide in your heart how much to give. And don't give reluctantly or in response to pressure. 'For God loves a person who gives cheerfully.'"[2]

Wait. Does the Bible actually say to not give reluctantly or because we feel pressured? Does it say we are to give *cheerfully*?

Yes. Yes, it does. At the grocery store or anywhere else.

THE CHEERFUL GIVER

My sister was just starting her junior year of college. She was using my parents' antiquated desktop computer for her homework and had been wanting a laptop for many months. Her birthday was coming up, and even though she wasn't asking for a laptop, I knew how much she needed one.

Money was tight, though. Linda and I were newlyweds living on $45 a week for food with zero extra funds lying around. I didn't have $500 to $1,000 to drop on a laptop for my sister. Even though I was short on money, I did have time and a willing heart.

I began driving all over town from garage sale to garage sale, looking for a winner. After coming up empty numerous times, I finally found a great laptop. It was only a couple of years old, had great specs, and was in great shape, and to my amazement, they wanted only $75 for it.

I took it home, cleaned it up, and bought a laptop bag for her to carry it in. I was ready for the big day. Linda and I were giddy with anticipation as we wrapped it. We knew how much this simple gift would mean to my sister. And we were thrilled that we got to be part of getting this blessing into her hands.

I will never forget the expression on her face when she opened the gift. It's forever etched in my memory. I'm not an overly emotional guy, but this moment really got me. To this day, it remains one of my favorite moments of giving, and it was the first time in my life when giving was more fun than receiving. And I wanted more of it.

PHOTO © BOB LOTICH

This unforgettable moment had nothing to do with the cost of the gift but rather was a combination of a few key ingredients. A true desire to bless her, God providing "seed for the sower,"[3] an essential need being met, and an overwhelmingly grateful recipient. These elements converged in a moment that helped me tear down the false beliefs I had about giving and reimagine what giving could be like.

SCIENTIFICALLY PROVEN TO MAKE YOU HAPPY

Not that we need scientific proof, since Jesus said it Himself—"It is more blessed to give than to receive"[4]—but I always love when science proves concepts that have been in our Bibles for thousands of years.

Numerous studies have proved that giving results in higher levels of happiness compared with receiving. One of the most extensive studies occurred over the course of five years and surveyed 2,000 Americans. The results were fascinating. The evidence revealed that consistent givers

- are happier than ungenerous people
- suffer fewer illnesses and injuries
- live with a greater sense of purpose
- experience less depression[5]

So, there you have it. Giving is kind of like a miracle drug.

A few years later, we had some friends come stay with us for the weekend. We knew that they were struggling financially. But we didn't know to what extent and certainly didn't know they had been praying for a financial miracle.

As they were packing up to head home, we asked them to join us at our kitchen table. Linda and I shared that the Lord had put them on our hearts and we felt Him leading us to give them a financial gift.

It was an order of magnitude greater than the laptop. In fact, at that point it was probably the biggest check we had ever written. I had never done anything like this and had no idea how it would be received.

I nervously slid the check across the table. When they saw the dollar amount, they burst into tears. This check was far more significant to them than we ever could have realized. As they shared more of their story, Linda and I began tearing up.

This was so much more than money. We were realizing it was a significant miracle in their lives. Not only did we have a front-row seat to what God was doing, but we also got to be key players in the miracle.

I can't adequately describe how satisfying it is to give something like this. To actively participate in a miracle that God is doing in someone's life. It has to be one of the greatest joys in life. And unforgettable moments like these truly make giving addicting.

It was in this moment that we realized this was what we were born for. This was how we wanted to spend the rest of our lives.

> LINDA: While those were a couple of special moments, I've found that they are available to us a lot more than we realize. Over the years, God has allowed us to experience many more remarkable moments like these. And this is why we save and earn all we can. So we can continue to be part of the miraculous things God is doing.

If I take an honest look at all those incredible moments of giving, a few things are worth noting:

1. **It had nothing to do with the amount of the gift.** Some were big; some small. It didn't matter, though. The joy we experienced was not based on the size.

2. **It stemmed from a willing heart, never from obligation.** None of these moments were times when I felt obligated to do what we did. While I might feel an obligation to get my sister a gift on her birthday, I certainly didn't feel an obligation to buy her a laptop. She would've been happy with a Starbucks gift card. We just wanted to do more.

3. **It almost always involved us giving more than was expected or giving with more intention.** Putting thought into a gift and really understanding your recipient's needs and desires greatly increases your odds of creating an incredible experience.

I believe God desires for everyone to have moments like we experienced with my sister and our friends. Actually, I don't just believe it. I *know* it. Because God Himself says He loves a cheerful giver.

> The adventure and joy of giving provides a far better motivation than guilt or shame ever could.

The adventure and joy of giving provides a far better motivation than guilt or shame ever could.

LINDA: Think of someone you love buying gifts for. For me, it's my kids and Bob. At Christmas, I buy too many gifts. It's hard to stop myself! Why? Is it because I feel guilty not giving them more and more gifts? No, it's because I'm so grateful for them. I want to bless them as much as I can.

That's what giving should feel like. Overflowing gratitude. When giving and gratitude combine, everyone is happy. You are blessed because you get to bless someone you love. That person is blessed as a recipient. And I bet God's heart explodes the same way mine does when my children share with each other.

CHAPTER 20

WHY WE BEGAN
"GIVING OUR AGE"

O n a cool spring morning, I was walking high up on a hill—a plateau of sorts—spending time with God and praying in my secret spot. Well, it wasn't really that secret. It was technically a construction site set aside for an upcoming phase of our subdivision. But it was a secluded area where I could go to think and pray. I liked to think of this place as God's treat to me.

As I walked with God in that field, I told Him about some of my big financial goals. The biggest one being that I longed to get our mortgage paid off and be 100% debt-free. According to my plan, it would take three or four years to pay it off.

Linda and I had been tithing for years at this point and even gave a little extra sometimes. In our minds we had reached the "finish line" of Christian giving. And, just like a Pharisee, I was proud of it. I had given God His 10%, and I had 90% to do with what I wished.

If I'm honest, I kind of thought that God owed me. I had checked the "good Christian" box by tithing, and now He should give me all the stuff I wanted. But what happened that morning, high up on the hill, forever changed my understanding of giving.

Though it wasn't His audible voice, God spoke to my heart that if we really wanted to see Him move in our financial life, then we should begin *giving our age* as a percentage of our income.

I was 31 at the time, so this meant 31% of our income. *Wait. Where did that come from? I've never seen that in the Bible. Who does this?*

As this thought lingered in my heart, I began trying to figure out whether this was even possible. *I don't know if we'll be able to pay the bills and buy groceries. And what about our plans?*

THE ADVENTURE

We had spent years dreaming about being 100% debt-free. We had been working toward that goal but just needed God's help to get there quicker. However, instead of helping pay off our mortgage, He seemed to be asking us to put our debt-payoff plan on hold and give instead, essentially turning that three- to four-year plan into about a 10-year plan since we wouldn't have any extra to pay toward our mortgage.

It made no sense. Yet here God was—not twisting my arm or using guilt or shame—but gently inviting me to go on an adventure with Him. Asking us to increase our giving from a little over 10% to 31%. It was a scary thought.

In this moment I recalled one of my favorite verses: "We know that God causes everything to work together for the good of those who love God and are called according to his purpose for them."[1] As usual, God's Word brought peace to my heart and reminded me of these three truths:

1. **God wouldn't ask us to do this unless there was something really cool attached to it.** God isn't into making requests just for fun or to make our lives difficult. He is always at work doing something awesome, inviting us to participate in it (in this case through giving). We just can't see how it's going to work out yet, and that makes it scary. But when we step back and trust that He is going to work it out *for our good,* we have the opportunity to enjoy even difficult moments of giving.

2. **Giving is an eternal wealth transfer.** We are eternal beings who are visiting earth for just a short while. Our earthly cur-

rency and possessions will lose 100% of their value when we make our way to our true home in heaven—unless we send them out ahead of us by converting them to an eternal currency, just like the fair tickets. Giving isn't just about losing something dear to us today. It's about investing for the future.

3. **It's all His anyway.** I've come to think of it like this. Say you hired me as your financial coach and we meet weekly during lunch. One week I ask you to grab lunch for us from Chipotle, my treat. I Venmo you $100 to cover it. We both understand that it's my money and I'm asking you to do something specific with it. Right?

    If the total for lunch that week was $25, then I might tell you to hang on to the change ($75) to get next week's lunch. You now have $75 of *my* money in *your* Venmo account. Is it your money because it's in your account? No.

    I could change my mind, though. I might ask you to use that excess money to do something completely different from my original intent. I might direct you to buy a burrito for the homeless guy on the road, buy our lunch for the next three weeks, or even spend it all on yourself.

    It doesn't really matter what I ask you to do with the $75 in your account, because it's *my* money. You're merely holding it in your account and waiting on my instruction.

> Giving isn't just about losing something dear to us today. It's about investing for the future.

As God's stewards, *all* we have is His. Our stuff, our bodies, our time, our kids, and, yes, even our money. It's *His* money that just happens to be sitting in our accounts right now as we wait for the word on how to use it (remember, this is why we call it Assets Under Management).

> LINDA: It took me a while, but I started to realize that when we're blessed, it's not always for us. Like Bob talked about in the Chipotle example, the money was never intended just for me; some of it was intended for someone else.
>
> We're blessed in order to be a blessing. When we understand that everything we have comes from God, it's a lot easier to send it where it needs to go. Money can just flow through us because we know it's not all purposed for us. That's one way we get to be God's hands and feet on earth.

Once I better understood these three truths, it was easier (though still not easy) to step out in faith as God invited us into some big giving challenges. During this particular invitation to give 31% of our income, I clung to Matthew 6:33: "Seek *first* his kingdom and his righteousness, and all these things will be given to you as well." I could have never dreamed what that would mean for us in the year that followed. Blessings far beyond what I ever thought possible.

Remember how we longed to pay off our mortgage? Well, after increasing our giving percentage to 31%, we paid off our mortgage and became 100% debt-free within just 10 months! Not the 10 years I was estimating, but 10 months. Yes, you read that right. We gave nearly three times as much and still reached our goal many years ahead of our plan.

In our finite minds, this didn't make any sense to us. It looked like we were going in the opposite direction of our goal, but God's ways aren't like ours. Following God helped us reach our financial goal so much faster than we could have dreamed, although human logic says it should have held us back. At the same time, God gave us the opportunity to experience more amazing giving stories like I shared in the previous chapter.

Follow God's leading. He is inviting you on an adventure, through the fear, through the impossible, telling you with a glint in His eye, *You can trust Me. I've got you.*

GOD'S INVITATION

Whenever God is leading me to give in some uncomfortable way, I feel a sense of anticipation and hope. That doesn't mean some things aren't scary—because they often are—but within that is a deep peace and comfort from God.

Now, I'm not saying that *you* should give your age like He asked us to do. But I'm saying, alongside the apostle Paul, that each of us should give what we have *decided in our own hearts* to give.[2] It's going to look different for each of us. Amounts, percentages, to whom, and when are all likely to be different.

> LINDA: The longer I live, the more I realize how individualized God makes our lives. He is far too creative to tell the exact same story twice. He's always got something new. And there is something completely new for you to live out. He invited us to give our age, but we urge you to seek the Lord for what He has for you! Never compare your story with what you see someone else doing. God has ideas in mind just for you!

Through the years, Linda and I have grown a collection of stories telling the miracles that God has done. Sometimes we get to see the recipient face to face, and other times we don't. But either way, we know that God is orchestrating miracles in other people's lives that we get to be a part of. He has created priceless memories for us and turned ordinary days into adventures.

God is sending the same invitation to you. A simple invitation to do something bold, something incredible, something exciting. To walk into the unknown with God. To fully trust in Him to provide and work miracles. To live as if you live only once. To live as if the fair is coming to an end soon.

CHAPTER 21

GIVING IS LIKE GARDENING

Let's pretend you're stranded on Mars. All you have is a little freeze-dried food and a dozen potatoes. How long do you think you could survive?

If you eat all the potatoes, you probably could make it a month. Or two. Max. Then you learn that a rescue mission is on its way but it'll take 18 months to arrive. How do you survive in the harsh Mars environment for 18 months with only 12 potatoes?

Instead of eating all 12 potatoes, you could plant them. That simple act could result in a harvest that would feed you and give you more potatoes to plant. A one-time decision to plant could make all the difference to your stranded-on-Mars-with-no-other-options self.

If you read the book or saw the movie *The Martian,* you will know this is essentially the plot. Mark, from the story, plants potatoes and survives until rescuers arrive. He wards off starvation not by eating first but by planting first.

And when giving seems like the last thing you should do, it's often exactly what you need to do to set things in motion.

THE WIDOW'S LESSON

In 1 Kings 17, we find an eerily similar story. During a severe drought, a widow had nothing left but "a handful of flour in a jar and a little olive oil."[1] Her plan was to make some bread as her and her son's last meal and then die.

At the same time, Elijah was running for his life. He had no food or water left in his hiding place, so the Lord sent him to visit the widow. When he arrived, Elijah instructed the woman to first make him a loaf of bread, then make one for herself.

I mean, who would do that? From the world's perspective, this is offensive. Who would ask such a thing of someone so destitute?

The answer is someone who understood how God does things. He knew that the way out of her situation was by *giving*, not consuming.

When the widow shared that she had only a small amount of supplies, the word of the Lord came to Elijah. God promised her that the supplies would not run out until He sent rain to the land. With God's promise to sustain her, the widow did as Elijah asked.

Because the widow followed the Lord's direction, the Lord made good on His promise: "There was food every day for Elijah and for the woman and her family. For the jar of flour was not used up and the jug of oil did not run dry."[2]

LINDA: I find this story fascinating. If you look at verse 9 of 1 Kings 17, you see that God told Elijah that He had instructed a widow to provide for him. Why would God send Elijah to get food from a home where there was no food?

It may sound unusual, but it's really not. Over and over we see God using the tiny amount we have and our willingness to obey. The widow could have said no. But if she had done that, she would have missed her miracle. She and her son would have died. But she said yes to God! She obeyed, and it saved her and her son's lives!

Maybe you feel the desperation she felt. Like things are over for you. But I want to encourage you today. God has a way out! Trust His instruction. If He's asking you to give, then a miracle is waiting on the other side. You can trust Him.

SEEDTIME AND HARVEST IS GOD'S DESIGN

Long ago, God promised that four things would always exist on the earth: "seedtime and harvest, cold and heat, summer and winter, day and night."[3] What intrigues me most about this list is that first one: seedtime and harvest. Boiled down, when you plant a seed, it will grow and you can reap the harvest. The first step, though, is to plant the seed.

This timeless principle applies to almost everything God creates and initiates. You might recognize it from the New Testament when Paul said, "Whoever sows sparingly will also reap sparingly, and whoever sows generously will also reap generously."[4] And guess what? Paul wasn't giving us a farming lesson. In this context he was specifically talking about giving.

Paul made it plain and simple for us: we reap what we sow with our giving.

This is exactly why the widow was invited to give (sow) when she desperately needed a harvest. In my own life I have seen this play out repeatedly. God leads me to give when it seems like the last thing I should do. He extends that gentle invitation to sow in order to reap a much-needed harvest.

THE PURPOSES OF HARVEST

While it's important to give, not all our income is meant to be given away. It's also not meant to be spent solely on ourselves. Paul broke this down in 2 Corinthians 9:

God is the one who provides seed for the farmer and then bread to eat. In the same way, he will provide and increase your re- sources and then produce a great harvest of generosity in you.

Yes, you will be enriched in every way so that you can always be generous.[5]

> # We are created to be conduits. The blessing is meant to flow through us to the world around us.

Some of our income is bread for us to eat. And some of our income is seed to be planted through giving. We are not meant to keep all the blessing. Instead, God blesses us with a harvest in order for us to be a blessing to others. We are created to be conduits. The blessing is meant to flow through us to the world around us.

GIVING PRODUCES BLESSINGS

You probably have, like me, seen people pervert this idea by "giving just to get." As if God is nothing more than a slot machine or a genie granting us whatever we desire. Or that the blessings of the Lord are somehow equivalent to materialism.

One of the greatest ploys of the Enemy is to take a biblical idea, twist it, and then get people to not only dismiss the counterfeit but also dismiss the truth. The devil is so bold he even tried to use this on Jesus.

"If you are the Son of God," he said, "throw yourself down. For it is written:
> *" 'He will command his angels concerning you,*
>   *and they will lift you up in their hands,*
>   *so that you will not strike your foot against a stone.' "*[6]

Jesus was no fool. He knew the truth behind the verse and used another as a shield against the devil's attacks: "It is also written: 'Do not put the Lord your God to the test.'"[7] Even though verses are used out of context—and often as weapons—the true message of the verses remains.

Likewise, while people will certainly pervert verses about giving in order to chase after materialistic desires, the biblical truth will always remain that giving produces blessings and we reap what we sow.

NEXT-LEVEL HARVEST

Harvest of all kinds is meant to bless others and provide more seed, which produces a harvest and even more seed to be shared. It's God's plan for proliferation. Paul described it this way: "He multiplies the seed as you sow it, so that the harvest of your generosity will grow."[8] And if we let it, the cycle just continues.

I love how Pastor Charles Stanley puts it: "You reap what you sow, more than you sow, and later than you sow."[9]

R. G. LeTourneau is widely considered to have been the world's greatest inventor of earthmoving equipment.* During his life, he famously gave away 90% of his income and lived on 10%. When asked about how he maintained such a steep giving curve, he was reported to have said, "I shovel out the money, and God shovels it back—but God has a bigger shovel."[10]

Many times when I had an increase in resources—a raise at work, a stimulus check, a year-end bonus, or some other unexpected in-

---

* Linda had no idea what earthmoving equipment is, so if you don't either, think bull-dozers and other big machines like that.

crease—I just assumed it was all for me and kept it all. Looking back, I realize that these were missed opportunities to plant seeds (and still have some extra for myself).

On the flip side, when I've recognized the opportunity and given, I've found that LeTourneau was right. It doesn't matter how much I shovel out; God's shovel is always bigger.

> **LINDA:** There's a beautiful picture here that I don't want you to miss. Can you imagine using a shovel to distribute dirt while a dump truck backs up behind you with a new load? It feels poetic and awe-inspiring. There are no limits on God! He'll take us as far as we'll let Him.

TRYING TO OUTGIVE GOD

Like so many other Christians, bestselling author Francis Chan grew up believing that giving 10% was the end goal.[11]

For years he gave 10% and occasionally a little more, but he says the real change happened after he went to Africa for the first time. His heart ached for the people. He connected with them on a personal level. They became his friends, his brothers and sisters who he loved. And it was out of this abundance of love that he wanted to give.

When Chan came home from Africa, he decided to see how much he could really give. He and his wife started looking at their finances to see what was possible. Driven by his love for the people he had met, he told his wife, "You know, honey, let's just see how much we can give away. Let's just figure it out. Let's start selling things. Let's go nuts on this." As time went on, Chan and his wife started to notice a correlation between their giving and God's blessing. He says that as they increased their giving, "the Lord just blessed us more and more."[12]

The following year, Chan sensed God leading him to give away $50,000—about equal to what he had earned the previous year. By

God's grace he was able to do it. The year after that, Chan sensed the Lord leading him to give away $100,000. While his salary wasn't even close to that amount, he decided to go for it anyway. Sure enough, God came through, and Chan met that $100,000 goal.

The next year God stretched his faith even further as he felt led to give away $1 million. He was shocked to the core, after all, how could he possibly give away so much when he didn't even make that much? Think about this: here was a man who just a few years ago didn't even make $40,000 a year, and now God was asking him to give away $1 million. Chan forged ahead in faith, and sure enough, God delivered.

There is no limit to what God can do, my friend. He can work miracles through us all, even if, like Francis Chan, we feel like unlikely candidates. Remove all the limits you've been putting on God. Take a moment, and ask Him to open your eyes to any increase He brings to you—no matter the amount. Commit to using the extra funds as the opportunity it is: a way to plant more seeds and begin increasing your harvest. What do you say?

CHAPTER 22

THE DANCING GORILLA

In a 2013 Harvard Medical School experiment, radiologists were asked to detect lung nodules.[1] Basically, they were asked to do what they did all the time: examine some CT scans and look for abnormalities in the lungs. On the next page is one of the scans they evaluated, which was actually much larger in person than what's printed here. See anything unusual?

Did you see the dancing gorilla?

In the experiment researchers added a matchbook-sized dancing gorilla to one of the images. The gorilla was 48 times the size of the average nodule. The purpose of the experiment was to see how many of the radiologists noticed it.

Let's just think about this for a minute. Not seeing the gorilla is like going into your bedroom to look for a sock and not noticing an extra mattress lying on the floor. It's like walking around a car you're renting to look for scratches and not noticing that half the door is torn off. Or looking for nail pops in the drywall and not noticing a soccer-ball-sized hole in the wall.

You get the point. It's beyond comprehension how people could simply not notice something right in front of them that's this much larger than what they are looking for.

Now, can you guess what percentage of the radiologists did *not* see the gorilla?

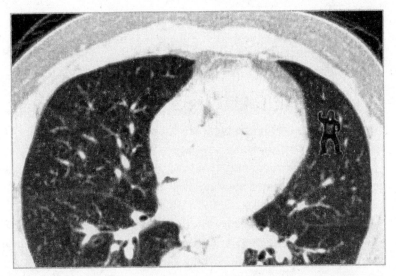

Source: Trafton Drew, Melissa L.-H. Võ, and Jeremy M. Wolfe, "The Invisible Gorilla Strikes Again" in *Psychological Science* 29, no. 9 (July 2013): 1848–1853, copyright © 2013 by Trafton Drew, Melissa L.-H. Võ, and Jeremy M. Wolfe. Reprinted by permission of SAGE Publications.

83%.

83% of radiologists in the study did *not* see the gorilla. And because they used eye tracking, researchers could see that, of the radiologists who didn't identify the gorilla, most looked right at it.

On top of that, these were radiologists! Not only did they go to medical school; they did an additional five years of training to specialize in their field. And since radiology is one of the highest-paying medical specialties out there, it attracts some of the brightest medical minds.

The point is, these are very talented, gifted, and persistent individuals. Yet in this study, 8 out of 10 of them didn't notice the dancing gorilla right in front of their faces. Why didn't they see the gorilla?

It's simple. They weren't looking for it.

They were going about their days, doing the things they normally did, and looking for only what they expected to find. See, when radiologists are looking for tumors, they are looking for a particular shape or pattern based on what they have learned and what they have seen in the past.

We often live our lives like radiologists do their jobs. We look for God to show up in particular ways based on what we have learned and what we have seen in the past. Much like God surprised the world by coming in the form of a baby, He shows up in all sorts of unexpected, undetected, and unbelievable ways.

As soon as the researchers told the radiologists to look for the gorilla, they each immediately saw it. The difference wasn't a matter of what was there. It was a matter of what they were looking for.

So it is with God's blessings in our lives. God is always lavishing us with blessings. The truth is, if we aren't looking for them, we don't see them. But that doesn't mean they aren't there.

BLESSING BLINDNESS

One of the biggest sources of my own "blessing blindness" is my fantastic ability to identify something as a coincidence or explain it away as a natural occurrence rather than something God had His hand in.

"Well, that promotion wasn't really a blessing, because it was a result of my hard work." Or "That check that showed up out of the blue was something that was actually owed to me, and it was just a coincidence that it came now." Or "Getting pregnant wasn't really a blessing from God; it was just that we found the right doctor to help us."

I have to remind myself that God often does the supernatural through surprisingly natural means. But missing God's blessings isn't a new problem. Even the Pharisees—who you would think would've been a little better at recognizing Jesus, given their knowledge of Scripture—completely missed Him when He stood directly in front of them. How is that for blessing blindness? They had been waiting their entire lives for Him to appear. And now they literally were standing face to face with God embodied in a human form, and because it was a supernatural blessing delivered in a natural package, they missed it.

It can be so easy for me to explain away the miraculous blessings God has deposited in my life. Even when they are 48 times bigger than everything else. Even when I'm looking right at them.

But the more you and I practice looking for God's blessings, the more we'll see them—just like Jeeps on the road.

IT'S A JEEP THING

A few days after buying a Jeep Wrangler, I was sitting at a stoplight and noticed this guy driving by, waving. And I mean *really* waving. I was racking my brain, trying to figure out who this guy was and how I knew him. I awkwardly waved at the last moment even though I didn't recognize him.

And then a few miles down the road, another friendly guy was waving. *Man,* I thought, *everyone must be having a good day.* And then it happened again less than 15 minutes later.

At this point I started feeling like Truman from the movie *The Truman Show* before he figured out that he was the unaware star of a reality TV show. I could not, for the life of me, figure out what was going on with all these oddballs waving at me all the time.

After days of this, I finally saw the common thread. All the people waving at me were fellow Jeep owners. It was then that I finally understood the old cliché bumper sticker: "It's a Jeep thing. You wouldn't understand."

Now that I knew what was going on and understood what it meant to be part of this club, I began watching much more closely for other Jeeps. I didn't want to miss my big moment when I would get to initiate my first Jeep wave.

I had never really noticed Jeeps before, but just by looking for them, I started to see Jeeps everywhere. And funny enough, my two-year-old daughter, in all her adorable enthusiasm, spots them too. From 100 yards away, she yells, "My Jeep!" I don't have the heart to tell her that not all Jeeps are hers, and you wouldn't either.

I'm constantly looking—with the help of an adorable rosy-cheeked beauty—and we don't miss a single one. In fact, it's a rare day when we don't see a Jeep. Which got me wondering, Were there lots of Jeeps on the road before? Do people just love to drive Jeeps and I missed it until now?

Turns out, it isn't just "a Jeep thing." It's an actual phenomenon known as the frequency illusion (or the Baader-Meinhof phenomenon if you want to get technical about it). It occurs when the thing you've just seen, experienced, or found out about seems to crop up everywhere. "It could be a word, a breed of dog, a particular style of house, or just about anything. Suddenly, you're aware of that thing all over the place. In reality, there's no increase in occurrence. It's just that you've started to notice it."[2]

We have the same opportunity to experience the Baader-Meinhof phenomenon with God's blessings. His blessings are always there, but when we start looking for them, we'll start seeing them everywhere. Even though this phenomenon is referred to as the frequency illusion, when we begin seeing God's blessings, it isn't an illusion at all. What we're seeing is the purest form of reality, and it reinforces who He is. By recognizing God's blessings in our lives, we better understand His love for us.

> By recognizing God's blessings in our lives, we better understand His love for us.

And while I love that my eyes have been opened to all the waving Jeep owners around me, I'm infinitely more excited about becoming more aware of God's blessings in my life.

START LOOKING FOR BLESSINGS

When you start looking for blessings, remember that *blessed* doesn't always mean financially rich. And *rich* doesn't always mean blessed. Sure, when Jesus almost sank Peter's boat with fish, that provided a huge financial blessing.[3] And God does stuff like that. But to assume that God can bless us only through money is criminally shortsighted.

If you've ever dealt with a major health issue, gone through a rough patch in your marriage, lost a close loved one, been overcome by addiction, or faced countless other challenges, you know that no matter how financially blessed you are, it won't solve the problem.

When I was earning the most I ever had, I was struggling with the biggest health challenge in my life. And even though I would have thought that I would be thrilled by the financial blessing at that time, it was eclipsed by the fact that I felt terrible every day.

On the other hand, I've had seasons when there wasn't as much in the bank account as I would have liked but God seemed to provide a constant stream of blessings and miracles—much like manna to Israel in the wilderness.

God's ways are so much higher than our ways. To assume that the only way He can bless or provide for us is with our man-made currency is a tragic insult to how great our God is.

So, how do we know what to look for? What could God's blessings look like? As you scan the horizon of your life, look for the unexpected. Look for Him at work in the things that seem like coincidences and in the things that are going right. In my experience, God often delivers blessings in unexpected packages. Where is God doing something unforeseen in your world?

Some 2,000 years ago, Jesus told us that "it is more blessed to give than to receive."[4] For most of my life, I simply didn't believe Him. Then I started looking for God's blessings as we gave. The more I looked, the more I saw, and the more I realized that He was right all along.

CHAPTER 23

SECRETS OF SIX-FIGURE GIVERS

A round age 24, I was at a point in my life where I felt anything but successful. I was still in corporate America and felt like my career was a complete failure—nothing was working out. I needed another point of view, someone to offer wisdom and advice on how to get unstuck.

So I called Chris, an older friend from church who was successful and whose advice I respected. I'll call him a life coach—though he would never call himself that. We decided to meet for lunch at the Cheesecake Factory.

> **LINDA:** I'll bet part of his strategy was to prove to you that if you could successfully pick an item out of their 100-page menu, you could accomplish anything.

During our meeting, he got right to the point and said, "All right. What do you want?"

Caught off guard, I asked, "Are you talking about ordering food right now? 'Cause I've only made it to page 18."

With a smile, he said, "What do you want out of life?"

What a heavy question to start with. I didn't know. What did I want? He continued to drill me until I said sheepishly, "I guess I want to make more money so I can buy a house and be able to give more."

"Okay," he said. "We're going to create some five-year goals. How much do you want to make?"

Umm. Is it really that simple? I thought. *You just pull random numbers out of thin air and set them as a goal? If that's the case, then sure, let's just go crazy here.*

Even though it had taken me the past three years to increase my $30,000 salary by about $4,000, I went all in and replied, "Well, I want to be able to make $250,000 a year. That'd be really nice. It would be good for my family. I'd be able to better provide for them and give more."

He handed me a pen and a sheet of paper and said, "Okay—great. Write it down."

It's a weird feeling making goals that are so far beyond the realm of possibility that you have no idea how they could ever happen in your life. *Maybe I shouldn't write down my goals. What if I fail?*

My pen faltered. It was difficult to even write something so absurd. Even though everything in me screamed "This can't be done," I wrote it down anyway.

Then Chris said, "You mentioned giving. Do you have any giving goals for the next five years?"

Hmmm. I had never thought about this. *But since we're going crazy and just pulling out random numbers from thin air . . .* It was in that moment, in a corner booth at the Cheesecake Factory, painfully aware of my $34,000 salary, that I set a goal of giving away $500,000 over the next five years.

Except, when I said it out loud, Chris snapped at me. "That doesn't make any sense. You can't do that. You can't give away $500,000 on a $250,000 salary. Even if you reached your salary goal with a 635% raise tomorrow, then tithed on it for the next five years, you would only reach $125,000 by year five."[*]

Chris was right. Earning a $250,000 salary wouldn't guarantee

---

[*] Chris and I both assumed that I'd give away only 10% of my income. Clearly God had other things in mind.

that I could reach my giving goal. And while I didn't have a moral issue with trying to earn a higher salary, it just seemed like a loftier and more eternally focused goal would be to set a giving goal that, as a by-product, would yield a higher salary. But if I did actually reach that $500,000 goal, then it would likely mean that my income would rise considerably more than I'd hoped and I'd be out of the dead-end job I hated, which sounded pretty amazing.

So I kept my ridiculous giving goal.

As I walked out of the restaurant and into the parking lot, I felt so much dissonance in my heart and mind. This giving goal was something that I would love to reach, but everything within me was telling me that it was impossible. Sure, maybe other people could do that, but never me.

I don't have the skills. I don't have the connections. I don't have the career path. I found hundreds of reasons that it would never happen. In my own strength, I didn't have what it would take to reach these five-year goals.

But I did have God.

While I had no idea whether I had proved myself to be a steward trustworthy enough to handle $500,000, I had His assurance that "his mighty power at work within [me] is able to do far more than [I] would ever dare to ask or even dream of—infinitely beyond [my] highest prayers, desires, thoughts, or hopes."[1]

God is the creator of the universe, so if He wanted to use someone like me to do something like this, even that wouldn't be too difficult for Him. Right? I still had so many doubts and questions. But just the act of writing down the goals and opening myself up to the possibility of failure was a huge step of faith—perhaps just mustard-seed-sized faith but faith nonetheless.

IDENTIFY A GIVING DREAM

God has some awesome things He wants to do in our lives. But He's just waiting for us to believe they are possible. If you have some huge giving dreams in your heart, I encourage you to take that bold step and write them down. Even if you only have what seem like tiny goals, write them down. I'll remind you of one of my favorite verses: "Do not despise these small beginnings, for the LORD rejoices to see the work begin."[2]

If you have never put your giving dreams to paper and don't know where to start, then I'll ask you the same direct question Chris asked me all those years ago: What do you want? What has God put on your heart? And more specifically, if you could give anything, what would it be?

Do you feel the pull to give a specific dollar amount? Sponsor a child? Maybe God is leading you to start a non-profit, build an orphanage in a third-world country, or buy property to use as a pastoral retreat? Whatever giving dream the Lord has placed within you, write it down.

After you've written down your giving dreams, include your non-giving dreams and goals for yourself and your family. I've found that if we do the Father's business, He makes sure to take care of ours: "More than anything else, put God's work first and do what he wants. Then the other things will be yours as well."[3]

As you write down your dreams, don't worry about the how. Our job is not to figure out how everything will happen but to trust God. He knows how to make it happen. He's just waiting for you and me to accept the invitation.

LINDA: Once you have your list, don't stop there. Put it on your desk, on your fridge, or by your bed. Look at, pray for, and think about the things on your list often—no matter how absurd they seem. I believe that God places dreams in our hearts that only He has the ability to accomplish.

GET COMFORTABLE WITH AN IMPOSSIBLE GOAL

When I met with Chris that day at the Cheesecake Factory, Linda and I were broke. We had to get creative to find $20 to buy birthday gifts for friends. I felt this painful tension between wanting to give boldly and generously and having barely enough money to survive.

Your Kick-Start

Want to jump ahead and complete your related challenge? Go to page 219 for details.

I remember feeling like a fraud because I knew I could never reach these goals I'd written down. The whole exercise felt like making New Year's resolutions that would be forgotten in just a few weeks.

I get why Sarah laughed at God when He said she would give birth at 90 years old.[4] And I can imagine the pain Joseph experienced when he told his brothers about the dreams God had given him.[5] And what did Mary think when an angel told her she would give birth—as a virgin?[6]

When it's tough to scrape together $20 for a gift, it seems laughable to imagine giving $500,000. It just seemed so far beyond the realm of possibility that I didn't want to let my mind go there.

> LINDA: But our encouragement to you is to go there—with God. And don't think about what you could do now; dream of what you wish you could do. Even if it seems ridiculous.

When it comes to giving, "going there" will look different for each of us. Maybe it's giving 10% of your income, maybe it's giving someone a car, maybe it's giving away a million, or maybe it's sending your pastor on a vacation. There are an infinite number of ways for us to give.

At this point in our lives, "going there" looks like giving away 90% of our income. Given our current circumstances, it seems impossible. And that's a good thing. Because if I knew how it could happen, then it probably wouldn't be a big enough dream.

Mark Batterson says it like this:

> *I've found that when God calls us to do things . . . it's going to be bigger than you are. It's going to be beyond your resources, beyond your ability. Often, it will be beyond your education. But God just seems to love to use people that are unqualified, and so maybe a way of saying it is, that he doesn't call the qualified, he qualifies the called.*[7]

When your reality appears to be thousands of miles away from your dream, it isn't easy to even write it down. But I want you to do it anyway.

Write it down. Pray about it. And take action on it as the Lord leads you.

If it's truly a God dream, you won't be able to do it in your own strength. But keep the dream in the forefront of your mind, pray, and follow God, and years later, when you look back, you'll be surprised to see how far He's brought you.

CHAPTER 24

NET GIVEN: THE MOST IMPORTANT METRIC

Driving home from the Cheesecake Factory that day, I couldn't stop thinking about the five-year goals I had just set. That led me to wondering what lifelong financial goals would look like. And then I asked the question, *What would it look like to be a financial success in the scope of eternity?* As I thought about this, it dawned on me that eternal financial success would look far different from how the world defines financial success.

> As Christians, we should measure financial success not by what we accumulate but by what we give.

The world tells us it's in financial independence, having a couple million in your Roth IRA or 401(k), having a vacation house, or retiring at 40. And while there isn't anything wrong with those goals, if we're actually *eternal* beings who are on the earth only for a breath of time, it seems far smarter to store up eternal wealth in heaven than to focus all our efforts storing up as much wealth as possible on earth.

And if that's the case, then we should stop defining financial success the way the world does: by how much we accumulate. As Christians, we should measure financial success not by what we accumulate but by what we give.

Sure, I have bills to pay, kids to feed, and a wife who likes to go on vacation every once in a while. But, using the fair analogy, it would be woefully foolish to accumulate hundreds or thousands of fair tickets knowing they will soon have no value. Instead, I want to be thinking about financial success through the longest possible lens—the eternal. I just need a way to track it.

STICKER CHARTS, TRACKING, AND GIVING

Want to know one of the greatest parenting hacks? No one told us, but I want to tell you. We discovered that if we wanted our kids to *want* to do chores, all we had to do was throw a piece of colored construction paper on the fridge and call it a sticker chart.

Boom! This simple idea instantly took our six-year-old from constantly complaining about doing chores to literally asking to do more each day. Why? Everyone likes seeing progress toward a goal—even adults. And let's be honest—we're all kind of like six-year-olds stuck in bigger bodies.

Our son loved seeing that page fill up with stickers with each chore. The closer he got, the more excited he became. Remember Pearson's Law: "When performance is measured, performance improves. When performance is measured and reported back, the rate of improvement accelerates."[1]

When we added the chart to the fridge, he could instantly see his performance. It was no longer obscure. He could see exactly how many chores he had completed that day. It was staring him in the face every time he walked into the kitchen. He constantly had his performance reported back to him, and as a result, he began asking us for more chores.

How is that for living the parental dream?

We can use the same tactic to measure our financial success—not what we accumulate but what we give. I'm not suggesting you use a sticker chart to track your giving, but it's the same principle. We can track our giving using what I like to call our Net Given. Like AUM, this calculation is a simple math problem; it's literally just a running total of how much we have given.

To track it, all you need is a notebook or a simple spreadsheet.* For us, we just log the date, the type of gift, the recipient(s), the cost (or value), and the reason and keep a running total at the bottom of the cost column.

Date	Gift	Recipient(s)	Cost	Reason
4/13/22	Bought food, made and delivered meal	Tammy and Mike	$35	They just had a baby!
4/19/22	Bought a drink for the guy behind me at Starbucks	Not sure!	$6	
4/26/22	Tipped hotel staff	Hotel staff	$20	
5/1/22	Gave cash	Church	$200	
5/3/22	Took Grant out to lunch	Grant	$40	His birthday
5/8/22	Bought *Simple Money, Rich Life* for Tim	Tim	$15	

As simple as this sheet seems, it turned out to be a game changer for Linda and me. It made giving something to be tracked. And watched. And celebrated. Like I mentioned in part 1 when discussing Pearson's Law, when you track something, your focus is naturally drawn to it, and it improves. If you don't track it, you focus on it less and therefore have less chance of growth.

* You can get a free copy of our Net Given template at seedtime.com/ng.

As a bonus, I still get the number-nerd rush of seeing our Net Given increase over the years.

> **LINDA:** This was a huge change for us. It broke us out of the comparison trap because now we were running a different race.
>
> It didn't matter that our neighbors were all trying to keep up with the Joneses, the Kardashians, or anyone else; we were focused on something better. And having that number in front of us helped keep us on track with what was most important to us.

At first glance, this might seem like a self-congratulatory exercise, a way to pat yourself on the back. But we don't see it like that. We see it as a way to give God more glory. It's a running display of what *He* has been able to do through incredibly ordinary people like us.

When we started to track our giving, it offered us a renewed purpose for getting up each day. I'm no longer dragging myself out of bed in order to work just to pay the bills, put food on the table, or add more zeros to my bank account. I'm getting up each day and earning so I can have an impact on the Kingdom and change lives.

For us, tracking this number has made giving more fun. It inspires us to find new and innovative ways to give. And when we see the fruit of our giving, it motivates us to do more.

> **LINDA:** It definitely pulls me out of that mentality where I always want more, more, more! And it's actually really freeing to get rid of that way of thinking and instead focus on something that has more meaning and makes a lasting impact.

Once you begin tracking the most important metric, your Net Given, I believe your world will never be the same. Like us, you'll be more aware of the ways God has worked through you to bless others. You'll spark

Your Kick-Start

Want to jump ahead and complete your related challenge? Go to page 220 for details.

a fire in your heart to further His Kingdom and spread His blessings, and the effects will linger long after you're called to your heavenly home.

WHAT TO TRACK

Linda and I track everything we give. From donations to church, to birthday gifts, to supplies to host a baby shower, to meals for new parents. Pretty much anything that we give away. Of course, not everything can be quantified and put on the sheet. There are plenty of generous acts that we haven't been able to assign a number to, and that's okay. We add them anyway. We list everything as a way for us to stay focused on the most important thing: giving rather than accumulating.

NEVER SUPPRESS A GENEROUS THOUGHT

A few years ago, I came across a simple quote that has become a helpful guide when presented with opportunities to give:

Never suppress a generous thought.[2]

When a generous thought pops into my mind, it probably isn't random. And since the devil loves to steal, kill, and destroy,[3] it most likely isn't him urging me to offer kindness to someone else. I know the generous thought is probably the Holy Spirit trying to lead me down a path.

So when the thought of getting a random gift for someone, buying coffee for someone, or texting someone I haven't talked to in years comes to me, I don't suppress it. I run with it. And God never disappoints.

Linda and I have been attempting to live this out for a few years now, and we have seen so many amazing God stories. If you need ideas of where and how to give, pray and watch for generous thoughts that the Lord sends your way.

LINDA: Over 10 years ago, I felt a leading to hug a friend whose dad had just died. Now, almost every time I see him, he comments on how much that hug blessed him. A hug! It's amazing how we can change people's lives through one simple act of kindness.

HOW NET GIVEN AND AUM WORK TOGETHER

We continue to prioritize our giving goals over any other financial goals and want to see our Net Given grow each year. But we also continue to track our AUM (Assets Under Management). We've decided that Net Given is our #1 priority with our AUM being our #2 priority. Both important, but different.

Simply put, I think of Net Given as the metric to track for heaven—it's a way to track our progress in storing up treasures in heaven. AUM is the metric to track for earth—it's a way to track all that God has entrusted us with on earth.

LINDA: We want to see both numbers grow, because each has a purpose and value. But ever since we had the revelation that our "fair tickets" would be expiring soon, Net Given has been our highest priority.

Now, you would think these two numbers would be in direct opposition, right? If you give something away, you're taking it out of your assets. As a result, your AUM decreases. Basic math, right?

But, here is the mind-blowing part. For the past 15 years, as we have increased our Net Given by giving, our Assets Under Management has increased at nearly the same rate.

Look at the chart for yourself:

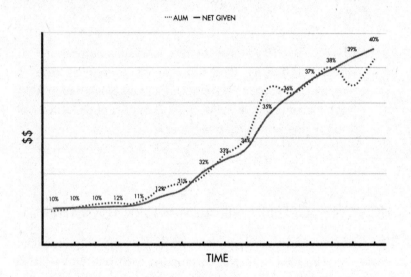

LINDA: This doesn't make any sense in the natural realm. Especially when you factor in that, most of those years, we were giving more than 30% of our income. But that's how God works! His ways are not our ways. It's been so fun to watch, but we would have never known if we hadn't tracked it!

And as we worked to seek first the Kingdom and His righteousness, God took care of all our needs.[4] We only needed to follow His calling.

In those years when our AUM doesn't increase, I'm not bothered, because increasing AUM isn't my primary focus. I view it as God shifting things around or testing us to see how we handle a down year. Will we still give when things aren't going as well as we'd like? I always want the answer to be yes.

MY MISSED GOAL AND THE BIG PICTURE

Five years had passed since my dinner with Chris at the Cheesecake Factory. I sat in my office, reviewing our Net Given sheet, and felt mixed emotions. I didn't meet my five-year goal. *Of course I didn't. $500,000 in five years? What was I thinking?*

But as I studied the past five years of giving, I saw the big picture of what God had done and I was overcome with joy. When we gave as God led us to, we became part of so many amazing moments: the tears of joy shared as we handed someone a check, the sigh of relief from new parents when we dropped off meals, the anonymous and unexpected gifts we got to deliver, the starving children we got to feed, the evangelism we got to fund, the widows we got to help support, and so much more.

These moments flooded my mind and filled my soul. I had no room in my heart to feel disappointed. We had been blessed to join God's work through our giving. Reaching the goal didn't even matter. It was the work that mattered.

Four years later, I was adding to our Net Given sheet. I glanced at the running total and saw we had crossed $500,000. I was overwhelmingly grateful for what God had done. This silly little goal should have taken the rest of our lives to reach, but He did it in nine years.

Of course, God wasn't done with the story. A few years after we crossed my initial goal, I was checking the numbers again, and my jaw dropped. He had taken it a step further and *doubled* my goal. Our Net Given had crossed $1,000,000.

Like the boy with the loaves and the fish, we didn't have much to offer. He certainly had no way to feed a crowd of 5,000, just as we had no way to give away a million dollars. But when we place what we have in the hands of Jesus, anything is possible.

CHAPTER 25

FOUR TIPS TO MAKE GIVING EASIER AND MORE FUN

I want to set you up for success with your giving. We have made plenty of mistakes over the years, so I want to share a few tips that have been a big help to us. Hopefully, they will help you as well.

TIP 1: GIVE FROM A GRATEFUL HEART AND A BROKEN HEART

We knew we wanted to give more, but Linda and I occasionally grappled with one question: Where do we give? I never thought this would be an issue. Shouldn't it be obvious who needs extra funds? Yet here we were. And we were not alone. Many givers struggle to answer this question.

Should you give to your church? Your cousin's GoFundMe? The homeless guy on the street? The preacher you love following on Instagram? An organization fighting sex trafficking? Something else? The options seem endless.

For years we struggled to narrow down where to give. But we began getting real clarity when we stumbled across some simple, helpful advice from Pastor Andy Stanley: "Give from a grateful heart and a broken heart."[1] While there are more ways to determine where to give, I have found this simple framework to be a great starting point.

LINDA: In other words, what people or organizations are you grateful for because they have blessed you? And what heartbreaking problems in the world do you want to see fixed?

What Are You Grateful For?

We're deeply grateful for the two amazing churches we've been part of over the past 15 years. No organization has had a more direct impact on our lives. Andy Stanley's advice just confirmed what we already believed about making tithing to our local church a giving priority. We want to ensure our church is able to continue its impact and remain strong and healthy into the future.

What are you grateful for? Is it your church, your children's school, a local non-profit that helped in your time of need? Or something else entirely? And what people are you grateful for? A simple compliment would be huge, but why not really hammer it home with some flowers as well? Or have them over for dinner to celebrate their birthdays? Or—one of my personal favorites—why not anonymously get them a gift you know will bless them?

Now let's talk about the second part of that giving framework.

What Breaks Your Heart?

Jesus often referred to the connection between our money and our hearts. It makes sense that we should give toward needs in the world that we desperately long to see met. One simple way we can help initiate change is by giving.

But we need to make a key distinction here because sometimes the line between a broken heart and guilt can get blurry. For example, there is a big difference between an organization using videos and images to inform us of realities we might not be aware of and that same organization laying on the guilt to pressure you and me to give. Remember, just as giving is a command for believers, so is *not* giving under compulsion. I love how Eugene Peterson paraphrases 2 Corinthians 9:7 in *The Message*:

> *I want each of you to take plenty of time to think it over, and make up your own mind what you will give. That will protect you against sob stories and arm-twisting. God loves it when the giver delights in the giving.*

It's easy to be led by the hurts present all around us. Or by whoever is yelling the loudest. But I believe our giving is most effective when we follow where God leads us. When deciding whether or not to give, I take time to pray about it and make sure I have peace in my heart as I give. If I feel like I'm being pushed or coerced into it, then I know I'm giving under compulsion.

What about you? What breaks your heart? What do you think is wrong with the world? Maybe it's human trafficking, maybe it's world hunger, maybe it's persecution of Christians in Iraq, or maybe it's one of any number of other causes.

LINDA: Bob and I were listening to a church member describe her story of human trafficking. We were both brought to tears as our hearts broke for the victims. I remember sobbing as I thought of the horrors children face every day. There wasn't any coercion or manipulation. We just received the information and immediately got a glimpse of how God must feel about it. It was something I couldn't get out of my mind. Over the following weeks and months, Bob and I talked and prayed about what to do. It had such a tremendous impact on us, and that's how we knew we had to do something. From that moment on, we were determined to use some of our financial resources to help.

Does something closer to home break your heart? Do you know a single mom who needs a break? Could you hire someone to clean her house? Or maybe you're friends with a lonely widow. Could you take her out for lunch? Who has God given you the means and opportunity to help?

GIVING TO PEOPLE VERSUS ORGANIZATIONS

I've had many conversations about whether it's better to give to a specific person or an organization. My best answer is both. There are pros and cons to each giving avenue. When giving to an individual, you often get to experience the moment with the recipient. You get to see the impact firsthand, and it can be deeply satisfying.

Organizations, on the other hand, tend not to provide that benefit but often do provide impact on a larger scale. For example, certain organizations can reach people groups in ways that I never could on my own. Some organizations pool resources to create something that benefits society— like Samaritan's Purse, Compassion International, or even an aquarium or zoo. And some organizations can use their size to influence public policy in a way that an individual couldn't.

The bottom line is that you can affect the world in different ways with each. I believe both have the potential to have significant eternal impact. So as you consider your giving, consider each path, and ultimately follow God's leading.

TIP 2: GIVE A PERCENTAGE

When John D. Rockefeller was earning $1.50 per week, which wasn't much even back then, he committed to give 10%. His commitment was not "I'll give 15¢" but "I'll give 10% of everything I ever make."

Because of that single commitment to give a percentage of his income, he found himself giving millions of dollars later in life. He said, "I never would have been able to tithe the first million dollars I ever made if I had not tithed my first salary, which was $1.50 per week."[2]

I know it's so tempting to believe that we will give more when we have more money coming in, but it never works that way. Parkinson's Second Law demonstrates that our expenses will rise to meet our income (translation: we will always spend what we earn) unless we have already put systems in place to prioritize giving.

For years my giving really happened only when extra funds were sitting in my checking account. Some months it would be a little, and other months there just wouldn't be any extra, so I didn't give. Not only was I not giving as much as I would have liked; it also always felt stressful.

I remember when I first made this decision to give a specific percentage each month. First, it made giving so much easier. I didn't have to think about how much I was going to give for the month—it had already been decided. Second, when I chose to apply the lesson from chapter 5 and make giving automatic, I never had to think about when or to whom; it was already in place. As a result, for the first time in my life, I was a consistent giver.

Last, I learned that if I committed to that percentage, then my giving would easily adjust to our income level for the month. I didn't have to feel good or bad based on the dollar amount that I gave, because my giving was based on a percentage. As a bonus, when my income went up, I stayed true to the percentage rather than the dollar amount, which effortlessly increased my giving.

If you aren't doing so already, prayerfully commit to give a percentage of your income. As you do, you will find that you're more consistently giving and it becomes far easier to grow the amount through the years.

Not a One-Size-Fits-All Rule

My rules for my kids regarding things like screen time and snacks are different because each child has unique natural inclinations, so I parent them differently. We have the same basic rules, but because I want to protect them, I give distinct instructions to each. I believe it's the same with God's instructions to us regarding giving.

Yes, as believers, we all have the mandate to give generously—but just because we use our age to determine our giving percentage doesn't mean you should. Just because the neighbor down the street gives 50% doesn't mean that I should.

Remember Paul's instruction: "Each of you should give what you have decided in your heart to give, not reluctantly or under compulsion, for God loves a cheerful giver."[3] You should feel no shame or guilt about your giving. Don't compare yourself with others. God loves you just as much as any of the most radical givers out there. We don't earn His approval by giving.

But I do believe that God invites you and me into this adventure with Him. It doesn't matter where you are on your journey. The way to the next level of giving is to continue taking steps in generosity, not to wait until you earn more. Keep moving forward. Give first; prove yourself faithful with little; then watch how God entrusts you with more.[4]

TIP 3: START A SEED ACCOUNT

Have you ever come across a GoFundMe campaign that you want to support but there's no money in the budget? Or maybe you forgot about a niece's birthday and now have no money to buy a gift. We've all been there. An unexpected giving opportunity pops up, but we struggle to find the money.

After agonizing over too many lost opportunities that God presented, Linda and I decided to start what we call a Seed Account. We created a category in our budget that we contribute to each month. The money in this account is used solely for giving. Nothing else.

It was a practical shift based on a spiritual truth (that it wasn't actually *our* money), and that made it so much easier to give. It was a two-minute game changer that allowed us to fully *enjoy* giving. We had always gotten joy from it, but when we created our Seed Account, it took our joy to a new level.

Your Kick-Start

Want to jump ahead and complete your related challenge? Go to page 222 for details.

LINDA: This was brilliant. Our money used to be in one big bucket, and we often had to decide between buying groceries and following a generous thought. That all went away with the Seed Account. When we set aside money in a separate category, it suddenly became easy to give and so much more fun. The money is just sitting there waiting to be spent. It's like spending someone else's money. And you have all the freedom to be as extravagant as you want!

WHERE WE GIVE

Linda and I have spent over 15 years gaining clarity on where to give the money God has entrusted us to manage. These percentages will most certainly change in the future, but this is where we've landed as of this book's publication.

It should go without saying that this is not instruction for you but rather inspiration. If you're one of those readers who likes to see specifics to generate ideas, then this is for you.

As we mentioned earlier, the Lord led us to this "give your age" framework for our giving. So, each year since, we've increased our giving by 1% (timed with my birthday). And in His divine wisdom, it has consistently been a good stretch for us.

At the time of this writing, we're giving away 40% each year. Here is how we break it down:

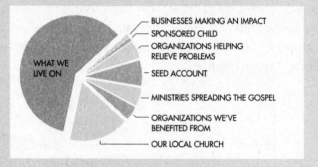

1. Giving from grateful hearts:

- 17% to our local church
- 4% to organizations we have benefited from
- 1% to businesses making an impact on the world (it costs more to buy a shirt not made with slave labor, so we consider the difference in cost to be an act of generosity)

2. Giving from broken hearts:

- 5% to ministries focused on spreading the gospel
- 7% to our Seed Account for spontaneous giving
- 5% to organizations helping relieve problems that break our hearts
- 1% to our sponsored child in Honduras

TIP 4: IMPLEMENT THE 50/50 RULE

You want to know the easiest way we found to increase our giving? Whenever we received a raise or an increase in income, we set up a simple rule to take advantage of this increase. It's called the 50/50 rule, and it works like this: when we get a raise, we split the increase evenly between living and giving.

Imagine you got a $500 per month raise. Most people would increase their standard of living accordingly. They might eat out more, increase their clothing budget, put more in savings, or even double the principal payment on a loan to pay it off sooner. What if you took a different approach, though?

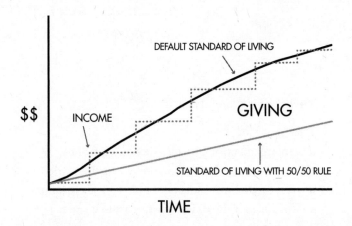

What if you raised your standard of living by only $250 and gave away the other $250? Wouldn't that still be a huge blessing? By limiting your monthly increase to half the raise, you could boost your giving without feeling that sacrifice at all.

When Linda and I have an increase in income, rather than letting our standard of living automatically increase, our goal is to continue to widen the gap between our income and our expenses. As we do, we have more opportunities to give.

Tim Mohns, a financial advisor, took an interesting approach. He decided to do a six-month experiment by capping his family's standard of living and giving away anything over and above. Like many of us, he wanted to see whether he could even do it.

Over those six months, Mohns would spend 15 minutes each day praying about where and how to give. He said that as he did, "that's where the adventure really began." After the trial period was over, Mohns concluded, "We are more free now financially than we've ever been. . . . More than ever, I have seen God's grace in my life." Mohns and his family decided to continue the experiment indefinitely.[5]

As many have said before, what if God prospers us not just to raise our standard of living but to raise our standard of giving?

CHAPTER 26

THE BUTTERFLY EFFECT

S cientists have described a crazy phenomenon commonly called "the butterfly effect" after the idea that air molecules disturbed by a butterfly's wings can affect the weather on the other side of the world several days later. Did you catch that? A butterfly could affect the formation of a tornado. (It's a real thing. You can look it up. Scientifically, it's called "sensitive dependence on initial conditions.")[1]

The butterfly effect applies to much more than just air molecules and weather patterns. One small change on the front end of a situation can lead to tremendous impact down the road. This includes one small generous act.

Let me prove it to you with a story I heard from bestselling author Andy Andrews.[2]

Years ago, a man named Norman Borlaug was named Person of the Week by ABC News. The reason? The network had determined that his hybridization of corn and wheat had saved over a billion people. Yes, over a *billion*.

But was Norman Borlaug the one ultimately responsible for saving those billion human lives?

Well, they wouldn't have been saved if it hadn't been for a man named Henry Wallace. Wallace served as the US vice president in the early 1940s. According to Andrews, "[He] used the power of that office to create a station in Mexico whose sole purpose was to hybridize corn and wheat for arid climates. And he hired a young man named Norman Borlaug to run it."

So, should Henry Wallace get the credit for saving those billion lives?

As it turns out, Wallace was mentored as a six-year-old boy by a student at Iowa Agricultural College. This brilliant student took young Wallace out on botanical expeditions and imparted a vision about plants' potential to benefit humanity. This student was none other than the agricultural scientist of peanut fame, George Washington Carver. He propelled Wallace toward developing plants for the good of the world.

The question I find myself asking is, What would have happened if Carver hadn't mentored little Henry Wallace? What would have happened to those billion people whose lives were saved?

It's the butterfly effect.

George Washington Carver had a massive impact on the world by developing over 300 uses for peanuts and over 100 for sweet potatoes.[3] But do you think he had any idea what tremendous impact that short mentorship of Henry Wallace would kickstart? When you think about the billion lives that were saved down the line, it's truly mind blowing.

> Until you get to heaven, you will never be able to comprehend the far-reaching impact of each and every act of generosity.

Today, as throughout history, every generous act has a butterfly effect, both in this life and in the life to come. Billy Graham seemed to understand this effect when he said, "In heaven I'll wish with all my heart that I could reclaim a thousandth part of the time I've let slip through my fingers, that I could call back those countless conversations which could have glorified my Lord—but didn't."[4] He knew that a short conversation or a simple gesture at one moment in time could make an eternal impact.

Friend, until you get to heaven, you will never be able to comprehend the far-reaching impact of each and every act of generosity.

THE KICK-START

PART 3

11. IDENTIFY A GIVING DREAM

(Read pages 194–97 for a refresher.)

Today we dream about the kind of impact you would love to make for the Kingdom of God. Don't focus on what you could do in your own strength. Instead, open your heart, dream big, and ask God for ideas.

Then spend five minutes thinking about how much it would cost for this dream to become a reality. Feel free to google "how much does _____ cost?" to find a rough estimate.

Remember, if it doesn't scare you a little, your dream probably isn't big enough.

○   Write down your giving dream here:

_____

_____

_____

○   What is your rough estimate of how much this dream would cost?

_____

12. CREATE YOUR NET GIVEN SHEET

(Read pages 198–205 for a refresher.)

Today your challenge is to create a document where you can track all the things you give. Think about tracking things like the following:

- buying coffee for a friend (or stranger) at Starbucks
- tithes and offerings to your church
- contributions to your favorite not-for-profit organization
- taking dinner to a new mom
- babysitting a single mom's kids

○ Start tracking your giving progress today. Use a notebook, create your own spreadsheet, or grab our Net Given template. Visit seedtime.com/ng to get a copy.

○ Set a monthly reminder on your calendar (or with Siri, Alexa, or Google) to update your Net Given sheet.

13. GIVE FROM YOUR HEART

(Read pages 206–9 for a refresher.)

Identifying where to give can be stressful. One of my favorite ways is by listing what I'm grateful for and what breaks my heart. So today that's what we're doing.

○ Make a list of organizations and people that you're
    grateful for.

_____

_____

_____

_____

_____

○ Make a second list of heartbreaking things happening
    in the world, in your country, in your community, or
    in your neighborhood.

_____

_____

_____

_____

_____

Spend 15 minutes in prayer and discussion with your spouse or
a friend if you need help forming these lists. If you identified a
cause but don't know specifically where to give, you can use a tool
like guidestar.org or charitynavigator.org to find organizations ad-
dressing those issues.

14. DECIDE ON A PERCENTAGE

(Read pages 209–11 for a refresher.)

If you don't currently give a consistent percentage of your income, let's change that today. If there is no number on your heart, then just start with 1% of your income this month. Do you already give a percentage of your income? Then prayerfully decide whether you're going to keep it the same or raise it.

Look at the lists you made on the day-13 challenge, and fill in the blanks below:

○   I am going to give ____% of my monthly income to

_____.

15. CREATE A SEED ACCOUNT

(Read pages 211–14 for a refresher.)

Today it's time to set up a Seed Account using your preferred budgeting system.

○   Create a budgeting category (and/or a separate bank account) for your Seed Account.

○   Write down how much you will transfer to the Seed Account each time you get paid:

_____

○   Schedule a reminder (or ask Siri, Alexa, or Google) to fund your Seed Account each time you get paid. Or better yet, set up an automatic transfer.

PART 4

ENJOU IT ALL

Wealth is the ability to fully experience life.
—HENRY DAVID THOREAU

Nothing beats fresh-baked homemade bread coming out of the oven. The aroma that fills the house is simply amazing. I've always loved it, so when Linda and I first got married, I decided to impress my new bride and learn how to bake bread.*

As you probably know, bread is made from a few key ingredients: flour, water, salt, yeast. But here's the thing: if you forget a key ingredient, then the end product is very different.

I learned this the hard way once when I forgot to add yeast to a recipe. At first, I thought it would be okay. I mean, the amount of yeast in a given recipe seems insignificant. However, I ended up with a brick of cooked dough that was inedible.†

If you've ever made this mistake, then you'll know firsthand how significant yeast is in making that perfect loaf. Linda and I have realized that it's the same with our formula. All four ingredients (save, earn, give, and enjoy) are needed to get the desired outcome.

So far, we've talked about how to save all you can, earn all you can, and give all you can. And now we turn our focus to the fourth part of the formula: enjoy it all. These four ingredients work together to help us achieve a rich life and significant eternal impact. But, as with the bread recipe, if you leave out even one ingredient, you probably won't get the desired result.

If we earn all we can just to store up treasures for ourselves on earth, we're shortsighted. If we give all we can but our spending is

---

* At this point I hadn't discovered the wonders of sourdough, so this was just "normal" bread.

† Not much food gets past me, but trust me, this was most certainly not edible.

out of control, we're missing out on a lot of opportunities. If we save, earn, and give all we can but don't enjoy any of the process, I believe we are missing out on the abundant life that Jesus promises.[1]

In 1 Timothy 6 (another fantastic chapter about giving), Paul said that God "richly provides us with everything for our enjoyment."[2] Did you catch that? Everything that God provides us is for *our enjoyment*.

We can enjoy our work, we can enjoy spending smart, we can enjoy the adventure of giving beyond our comfort zone, and we can enjoy the blessings, material and otherwise, that God has given us.

Just so there is no confusion, this part of the book isn't about elevating money's status as a source of joy in our lives. If we find ourselves seeking anything other than God as our ultimate source of joy, we will be disappointed. In his book *Mere Christianity*, C. S. Lewis wrote, "Nearly all that we call human history—money, poverty, ambition, war, prostitution, classes, empires, slavery—[is] the long terrible story of man trying to find something other than God which will make him happy."[3]

So, in this part we will explore how to enjoy the blessings of the Lord without fear, guilt, or shame. And how to enjoy some of the things that we often don't think of as enjoyable. Many people don't enjoy any of the previous three parts that we have discussed. They hate saving money, hate the work they do, and hate giving. But it doesn't have to be that way.

LINDA: It's true. You really can enjoy all three parts. And it should come as no surprise that when you enjoy your work, spend smarter, and have fun with giving, you want to do more of each!

And that's exactly what we're after.

CHAPTER 27

ENJOY WHAT PROGRESS
ACTUALLY LOOKS LIKE

I n 2005, Linda and I were broke. We had low incomes and a mountain of debt we desperately wanted to pay off. I was leading the fight to get out of debt and turn our financial lives around. It was up to me to convince Linda it would be worth it.

I remember trying to explain to her that, as hard as it was, it wouldn't last forever and that it would be worth it when we were debt-free. We would be able to save up a down payment for a house, give more, and travel more. All the things we both wanted.

We had to just give up some things first. As author John Soforic says, "The way to gain freedom is by temporarily giving up all freedom."[1] And we were doing just that—temporarily giving up a lot in order to get that freedom we longed for:

- We were newlyweds, but I was writing from 10 p.m. to 2 a.m. on the weekends, trying to get my blog off the ground to bring in a little extra income.

- Linda had been living at her parents' house with about $800 per month of disposable income before we got married. Now I was asking her to live on $50 per month of personal spending money.

- While we could have owned a house, we chose to live in an apartment.

- I was driving that 12-year-old bubble Taurus—rather than buying a new car.

All in all, we chose to make a lot of sacrifices. We didn't have to go that extreme, but I intuitively understood that the bigger the sacrifices, the quicker we could reach our goals and get to the other side.

Our path to debt freedom had many ups and downs. But I have come to understand that, regardless of the financial goal—paying off debt, reaching a savings goal or a giving goal, buying a house—progress tends to follow a similar path. When you understand how progress works, it's much easier to enjoy the journey.

THE FIRST PHASE OF FINANCIAL PROGRESS: VISION

Linda and I were in the first phase of progress, which I like to call the vision phase. I had a vision for our finances. A plan. All I had to do was implement it, put in the hard work, and watch the progress. Easy, right?

We tend to think that progress should be directly proportional to the amount of effort we put in. We also expect the amount of prog-

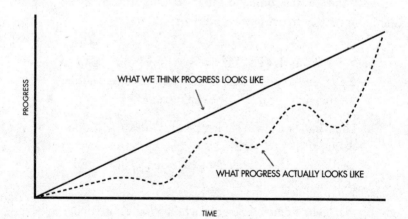

ress to stay consistent throughout the journey. But in reality, progress almost always looks very different from what we expect.

Many months, it was tough for Linda and me to stay motivated, particularly when an unexpected expense came up that reversed our progress. Here we were, making sacrifices to reach a goal, only to go backward.

I am reminded of habits expert James Clear's explanation of those moments: "In the early and middle stages of any quest, there is often a Valley of Disappointment. You expect to make progress in a linear fashion and it's frustrating how ineffective changes can seem during the first days, weeks, and even months. It doesn't feel like you are going anywhere."[2]

Have you ever been there? Struggling in the valley, unable to see how your effort is moving you toward your goal? Like Linda and me in that season, you need a different vantage point.

American newspaper reporter Jacob A. Riis writes, "When [nothing seemed] to help, I would go and look at a stonecutter hammering away at his rock perhaps a hundred times without as much as a crack showing in it. Yet at the hundred and first blow it would split in two, and I knew it was not that blow that did it, but all that had gone before."[3]

Think back to those moments of sacrifice. Can you relate to the stonecutter? I sure can. But when you understand the process, you can enjoy hammering away at that rock, knowing the split is coming—even when you don't see any progress. It's right around the corner.

THE SECOND PHASE OF FINANCIAL PROGRESS: MOMENTUM

There is one particular bank lobby I can so easily picture in my mind that I could paint it from memory. It was adorned in typical bank decor: dark cherry desks, cheesy wall art, and, of course, lots of beige. Even though it has been over 14 years since I last stood in that lobby, I can remember it like it was yesterday.

The reason? Because this was the bank lobby where we paid off our first car. The moment we handed the check to the teller will be etched into my memory for the rest of my life. For us, it was more than just paying off a car. It was the first milestone proving that the work—the hammering of the stone—was worth it.

We had reached the momentum phase, a tipping point of sorts, on our journey. We had put in the effort and made the sacrifices, and for months we hadn't seen results. Now we were starting to see the outcome of our struggles—the small apartment, the tight budget, the late nights. Our sacrifices were producing fruit.

Experiencing that win fueled our desire to keep going. It created momentum. Over the months that followed, we reached new milestones faster. We paid off all our credit cards, then my car, then my student loans. We loved watching our AUM increase as we paid off another debt, and we wanted more.

With each victory, the momentum increased. We began hitting huge milestones. We turned my blog into full-time income; Linda "retired" from her job to come help me with the business; we gave in ways we had only dreamed of before— all far quicker than we thought possible.

Your Kick-Start

Want to jump ahead and complete your related challenge? Go to page 250 for details.

That's the thing about financial progress; it typically requires more effort on the front end and less on the back end. At the beginning, it often doesn't go as quickly as you expect and there are more hiccups than you predicted.

But once you pass the tipping point, the opposite begins to happen.

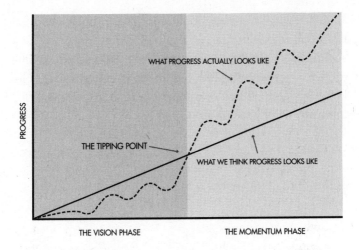

Things move faster than you expect and with less effort. It feels like the difference between walking uphill into a headwind and walking downhill with the wind at your back. Or maybe even roller-skating down.

In the momentum phase, it can feel like you're cheating because you put in less effort and still get considerably better results than before. The challenge is sticking with it through the vision phase. But once you know how this pattern works, you can begin to enjoy every part of progress because you know, once you reach that tipping point, everything is going to change.

If you're in the vision phase, hang in there; it's going to be so worth it: "Let us not become weary in doing good, for at the proper time we will reap a harvest if we do not give up."[4]

LINDA: If you're married and wanting to get your spouse on board, you could do some vision casting together. Sit down, and talk about all the things you two want to do in life, financial and personal. Your goals might include traveling, buying a vacation home, building a massive garden, golfing three times a week, or staying home with your kids.

Once you have your goals, share the progress chart in this book with your spouse. Explain how progress will look so you can both stay motivated while you sacrifice a little to reach your goals. This has to be a conversation. Get in on it together! You're a God-made team, after all. It's amazing what you can do together.

CHAPTER 28

ENJOY SPENDING

Some 700 miles northeast of Sri Lanka, there is a small island called North Sentinel Island. It's home to the Sentinelese, one of the few remaining groups of primitive people mostly uncontacted by the rest of the world.[1]

I often imagine that on the island there is a 40-year-old man like myself. Even though we both live in the 21st century, we were born into very different parts of the world. He likely lives off the land—hunting and foraging for food. Perhaps he comes home after a hunt and embraces his kids, but instead of having a game night, they tell stories under the stars.

Our lives are drastically different, so naturally we value different things. Since he is a hunter, he might sacrifice a lot to get a sharp knife, a bow, or a spear, whereas I have no use for primitive weapons because most of my food comes from Chipotle. On the other hand, I find a lot of value in having a car (mostly so I can drive to Chipotle), but since he is on an island with no roads, I don't think he would care much for it.

This point rings true across the world. We all value things differently. If you're married, you already understand this, right?

Now let's look at another example. Say Amanda spends $300 a month on a nice car. Many of us nod and think, *She might need a car to get to work (or Chipotle).** We see it as a reasonable expense.

---

* It must be getting close to lunchtime. I can't get their Barbacoa tacos off my mind.

Amanda's neighbor Stacy also spends $300 a month on a car. Then she learns about luxury ice (yes, it's actually a thing) and how much it affects the taste of her fresh-squeezed lemonade. Stacy decides to sell her car and ride a bike in order to fund her ice-connoisseur journey.

Spending $300 a month on *ice* probably seems insane to most of us. However, shouldn't Stacy be afforded the right to enjoy the thing she values—the ice that brings her joy—without judgment? Would you want to be given the same right?

The reality is that I have a house for my car (aka my garage) that keeps wind and rain out quite well. Meanwhile, there are people all over this world whose living conditions aren't as comfortable as my garage—where my car lives. My garage should be viewed as an extravagance, but because everyone around me has one, it seems pretty normal.

Whether it's a garage or something else, you can bet you're spending money on something that is an insane luxury to someone out there. I'm pretty sure my neighbors think I'm an idiot because I just paid $240 for a composting tumbler that is basically a big plastic cylinder full of dirt. And you can be sure someone somewhere thinks you spend money like an idiot too.

LET'S STOP JUDGING ONE ANOTHER

Even though I understand that this spending thing is all relative, I still occasionally find myself judging others' spending. *I mean, who would ever spend that much on [insert thing not that important to me but probably important to them]?*

But is it possible that each time we find ourselves judging how someone else spent money, we are guilty of seeing a speck in a neighbor's eye while having a log in our own eyes?[2] *Ouch. Guilty as charged.* And if extravagance is relative, then shouldn't we stop judging one another's spending habits?

Could it be that it's none of our business and simply between each person and God? If you recall, Judas Iscariot—a man who loved money so much that he sold out Jesus for a bag of silver—condemned Mary for pouring expensive perfume on Jesus's feet.[3]

Then we have Solomon's temple, which was created with so much gold that it would be worth over $200 billion today.[4] That seems pretty extravagant if you ask me, yet God provided the instructions for it.

What I take from these examples is that there is a time for sacrificing and a time for spending liberally. The key is to know when to do each and to refuse to make spending decisions based on what others think or say. Instead, our goal should be to please and honor our audience of one. Only one voice matters, and when we are in conversation with Him, we can turn off the guilt and enjoy His blessings.

THE KEY TO GUILT-FREE SPENDING

Let's just decide right now that we aren't going to feel guilty for spending money. I believe it's possible to enjoy what you buy without guilt or shame. Here's how we do this. We recognize that it's all God's and prayerfully manage the money entrusted to us to the best of our ability. When we keep our hearts tuned to God, we can spend guilt-free and enjoy the fruit of our labor.

> When we keep our hearts tuned to God, we can spend guilt-free and enjoy the fruit of our labor.

Remember, you can enjoy the giving and enjoy the spending because God "richly provides us with everything for our enjoyment."[5]

This can be a tough balance to live out. It's easy to spend all our money on ourselves and give no thought to what God would have us do as stewards. At the same time, it's easy to feel guilty about spending even a dime on something we would enjoy. While it is easy to go to either extreme, there is freedom when we walk in the balance.

One practical way Linda and I have stayed in balance is by putting distinct limits on our spending.* By limiting our spending in areas of temptation, we force ourselves to save for those indulgences. And when those accounts are full, we are free to spend the money as we choose.

Do you recall the Jeep I mentioned a few chapters back? Well, I had actually wanted a Jeep for many years. And even though we technically "had the money," it took me a few years to get one because that money was earmarked for other things—emergency savings, retirement savings, or giving. Instead, I saved up until I had enough to buy it with cash—without pulling from our other priorities.

Even though my flesh didn't enjoy waiting, I found this experience to be so good for me. It gave me an opportunity to trust God for the thing I was craving—rather than just making it happen in my own strength. I could have just gotten a loan and immediately satisfied my desire, but because I chose to trust my Provider, when the money was finally available, I was able to spend joyfully without a hint of guilt for this "extravagance."

It felt even better knowing that a percentage of our money was already set aside to give. I didn't need to feel bad for not giving the Jeep money to the local shelter or for not putting it into the offering bucket. It was already decided. This money was designated to buy a Jeep. Guilt-free.

The truth is that you can—and should—do both. Enjoy your giving and enjoy your spending.

Remember, it's all His. Let's ignore the critics. Let's prayerfully use money in ways that honor Him. Let's enjoy whatever we choose to spend money on.

---

* Remember chapter 7, where we talked about accountability?

CHAPTER 29

ENJOY WHAT YOU HAVE

John D. Rockefeller was one of the richest men to ever live.[1] At the turn of the 20th century, with his wealth, he could have it all. Right? But what if wealth wasn't measured by dollars, but by comfort, conveniences, and luxuries?

Think about it. What a few hundred dollars may buy today, millions of dollars couldn't have bought then. Today we have air-conditioning, airplanes, refrigerators, GPS, smartphones, and millions of other modern conveniences. But even with all his wealth, Rockefeller couldn't buy air-conditioning. Maybe he had 15 people fanning him on a hot summer day (because he could afford it), but I would still rather have air-conditioning. Wouldn't you?

> **LINDA:** Plus, he was probably stuck in a wool suit all day. Didn't even have shorts, poor thing!

He probably had drivers to take him by buggy all around town. And it was probably a Rolls-Royce of buggies with all the best features a buggy could offer. But I would much rather be riding in a 10-year-old Chevy. Wouldn't you?

If we change the way we think of wealth and compare our standard of living with Rockefeller's, we're doing pretty well. In fact, I would go as far as to say that the majority of Americans live an all-around more comfortable life with far more conveniences and luxuries than Rockefeller did. So, measured by this standard, who is actually richer?

HOW MUCH DO WE REALLY NEED TO BE CONTENT?

Did you know that if your annual income after taxes is over $33,000, then you are in the top 4% wealthiest people in the world?* (To put this in perspective, if you took 99 random people from around the world and placed them in a room with you, then 96 of them would be poorer than you while only three would be richer.)

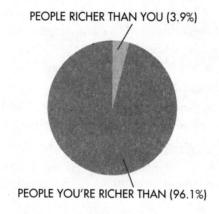

PEOPLE RICHER THAN YOU (3.9%)

PEOPLE YOU'RE RICHER THAN (96.1%)

How is it that we can be living more comfortable lives than 96% of the world's population and one of the richest men from 100 years ago yet still feel like it isn't enough?

Solomon hit the nail on the head when he wrote, "The eyes of man are never satisfied."[2] As the wealthiest man in his time, Solomon concluded that there was no end point where our desires would be fulfilled. Where we would say, "Enough. No more."

No matter how much we get, we always crave more.

---

* See for yourself at howrichami.org.

LINDA: If we turn our hearts toward the provision rather than the Provider, we have a problem. If we're more interested in the joy, contentment, peace, and security that we think will come from the things we own or want to own, we're headed in the wrong direction.

I can usually spot this in my own life when nothing can satiate my desire for more. But when I find my security in God, I can easily walk away from things I crave.

THE HARDEST FINANCIAL HABIT TO BREAK

I was recently asked about the most difficult habit to break when I started getting my finances in order. For me, it was the habit of discontentment. I used to see something I wanted, and I would crave it and scheme to get it, to the point that I would lose all my joy until it was mine.

Sometimes it was a physical object like a car or a house, and other times it was a respectable goal like paying off debt. But no matter the objects of our desire, if our contentment hinges on those things rather than Jesus, we're going to be disappointed.

> No matter the objects of our desire, if our contentment hinges on those things rather than Jesus, we're going to be disappointed.

My lack of contentment drove me to spend more than I earned. I was earning more than enough to live a nice life, but I wasn't satisfied with what I had. I wanted more and wasn't happy until I got the thing I was chasing. My joy hinged on that next goal or object rather than Jesus, and as a result, I was never satisfied.

In order to overcome my discontent, I had to identify it. Many people spend their entire lives chasing a moving target, not understanding this. For so long I was one of them. I believed that once I achieved or got the next thing, I would be content

- once I got my credit cards paid off

- once I got a Tesla

- once I got a bigger house

- once I earned $100,000 a year

- once I paid off my mortgage

The Enemy wants us to waste our lives chasing arbitrary goals, believing the lie that our contentment is contingent on our possessions or circumstances. All the while, he just continues to move the target, like in a game of whack-a-mole. As soon as we acquire the thing we believed would make us content, the next thing for us to long for pops up. And on and on it goes.

Your Kick-Start

Want to jump ahead and complete your related challenge? Go to page 251 for details.

I thought that getting what I craved would satisfy me, but just like drinking salt water, it only increased my desire. Only when I identified my sources of discontent was I able to contend with the Enemy.

THE "NO" MUSCLE

I've found that getting in the practice of telling myself no has been incredibly helpful in battling discontent. I still view it as a daily exercise—just like getting my 10,000 steps in for the day.*

---

* Let's be real. I have a home office that is about 25 steps from the kitchen. I'm pretty pumped when I break 3,000 steps in a day.

Each morning, I ask myself, *How can I tell my flesh no today?* It might be saying no to dessert until after dinner or saying no to Netflix and yes to opening my Bible app, or it might be saying no to responding to a comment that has me all riled up on Instagram.

Every time we say no to our flesh, we're strengthening that muscle.

By developing this habit, I began to be thankful and content. I was finally enjoying the things I had, rather than chasing after the newest toy on the market. If we're not programmed to get a new car every other year, a new wardrobe each season, or a bigger house to impress our friends, then it's much easier to find joy in what we have and spend less overall.

It has taken me a while to dismantle this habit of discontent, and while at times I still battle it, I believe this is one of the most important moves I've made in my financial life. I no longer have an insatiable desire for that next thing, so I no longer spend money to find temporary satisfaction. This progress has proved to be tremendously valuable.

THE HAPPY PILL

Imagine if the big pharma companies created a pill that increased happiness by 25%. You would see one of those ads with a happy family walking on the beach, and then you'd hear the voice-over say, "Side effects may include headaches, rashes, anger, violent outbursts, cruelty toward animals and plants, sudden urges to pick fights on social media, and in rare cases death."

Yet they would still go on to make billions with it.

LINDA: Please, let's not give anyone any ideas.

But what if there was a way to increase our happiness by 25% without taking a pill? Dr. Robert Emmons concludes that there is. According to his research, "regular grateful thinking can increase happiness by as much as 25 percent."[3]

Not only does the simple act of choosing to be grateful for what we have cause us to enjoy what we have; it also provides many other positive side effects. No headaches, no rashes, and no sudden urges to pick fights on social media. Just all the benefits.

Heather Craig, a psychologist in Melbourne, Australia, says, "Research on gratitude has shown that it is associated with positive emotions including contentment, happiness, pride and hope."[4] And the benefits actually go way beyond that. After studying more than 1,000 people, Dr. Emmons found that those who consistently practice gratitude experience a host of benefits:

- stronger immune systems
- lower blood pressure
- better sleep and more energy
- more joy and pleasure
- less loneliness[5]

What we see here is that there is an antidote to discontentment. While the temptation to feel discontent is likely to always be in our lives, we can overcome it. The secret is to be intentionally grateful for what we have.

PRACTICAL GRATITUDE

So, I'm all for being more grateful, but how? How can we practically live out gratitude? Today you can do two simple things that will help:

1. **Start a gratitude journal.** If you really want to go big, buy a gratitude journal and make it a daily habit to write in it. Or simply set a reminder for 10 p.m. each night, and write down three things you're grateful for.

2. **Make a list of 50 things you're grateful for.** Seriously, it's that simple. I remember receiving this marriage advice: write out everything you love about your spouse. I waited to do this exercise until Linda and I were in a particularly bad fight, which made it more challenging but also more effective. Instantly I went from seeing the enormity of the offense I was frustrated about to having a much more accurate picture of what I loved about her. It quickly dwarfed the offense.

LINDA: From now on, every time we have a fight, I'm going to hand you a piece of paper numbered 1 to 10.

CONTENTMENT, GRATITUDE, AND MONEY

As we shift our perspectives, say no to our urges, and actively seek out gratitude, we have more control of our finances. We no longer feel the urge to buy that new phone but are content with what we have for the moment.

Does it mean we shouldn't buy that new phone? No. But by finding contentment in our current phone, that new phone loses its influence over us. It isn't a matter of urgency, and as a result, it no longer holds power over our finances. We become the masters of our money—not the servants.

CHAPTER 30

ENJOY REST

In 2019, Christian Rasmussen, a real estate agent and personal friend, was attempting to sell a house. The house had been listed for over 40 days, and he had held an open house every Saturday and Sunday. During that time, he didn't get a single offer. So he decided to attempt something that most would say was impossible.

After praying, he felt the Lord leading him to take Sunday as a Sabbath day each week. That might be challenging for most of us, but it's even harder for real estate agents. In the real estate world, Sundays are reserved for open houses and chauffeuring clients around town to view properties. In fact, most of their work happens on the weekend. It's hard to imagine how Christian could stay in business by denying his clients such a valuable day.

Doubling the odds against him, he was still a rookie agent. He hadn't built his client base. He was advised by the veterans not to do it. In fact, he was told, "You will never make it in this industry if you do that."

But he had discovered something that so many Christians miss: "Remember the word which Moses the servant of the LORD commanded you, saying, 'The LORD your God is giving you rest, and will give you this land.'"[1]

God gives rest. God gives the land (or the breakthrough). Notice that He gives both. And both are to be enjoyed. Yet many Christians act as if rest shouldn't happen and definitely shouldn't be enjoyed. I mean, if you aren't working, you're lazy, right?

It's easy to believe that we have to work hard in our own strength to make anything happen. That it all depends on us and our abilities. And often, as a result, we don't dare rest.

LINDA: God gives us rest, but it takes faith to receive it. When presented with the idea of taking a Sabbath day each week, many seem to think that it just isn't possible. There is too much that needs to be done. And that kinda sounds like what lazy people do.

But what if God has set it up so that when we step out in faith by resting—even when it doesn't make sense—we actually get more done? Or maybe "getting more done" isn't the best way to say it; maybe "getting the right things done" is a better way to say it.

That's exactly what happened as Christian began this Sabbath experiment. Against all odds and veteran advice, he moved forward with his weekly rest day. The first Sunday came, and he didn't host an open house. He chose Sabbath rest instead. The next day, he received a full-price offer.

He continued to defy all conventional wisdom for real estate agents by taking a Sabbath rest each Sunday. To the surprise of all the veterans who thought it was a terrible idea, Christian's business just continued to flourish. Over the next couple of years, he had to hire staff just to keep up with the growth.

Chick-fil-A is another one of those anomalies. We all know that the stores are closed on Sundays and have seen success. But did you know that Chick-fil-A earns more per restaurant than McDonald's, Starbucks, and Subway—combined?[2] All while being closed on Sundays.

What if God has given you one day a week to rest, enjoy Him, and

> What if God has given you one day a week to rest, enjoy Him, and do literally no work?

do literally no work? To step away from the nonstop busyness of life and enjoy His goodness. To intentionally do away with all the *shoulds* and *have-tos* and instead just enjoy God and the precious moments of the day.

SABBATH IS AN ACT OF FAITH

For driven people like me, choosing to take a Sabbath day is often a pretty big act of faith. It can be terrifying—and sometimes even feels irresponsible—to intentionally do nothing when so many important things need to be done. And done right away.

But the Sabbath is an invitation to trust God with these things on our to-do lists. It's an opportunity to say, *God, this seems urgent and important, but I choose to let it sit until tomorrow and instead rest and enjoy this day that You have made. I choose to trust that You are fully in control and that You will work out all the things on my plate.*

You might use the same argument that I used for years when fighting against the idea of embracing Sabbath: *I don't deserve to rest until I get my work done.* But we both know the truth: the work is never done.

Author Mark Buchanan says this,

> The rest of God . . . is not a reward for finishing. It's not a bonus for work well done.
>
>   It's sheer gift. It is a stop-work order in the midst of work that's never complete, never polished. Sabbath is not the break we're allotted at the tail end of completing all our tasks and chores, the fulfillment of all our obligations. It's the rest we take smack-dab in the middle of them, without apology, without guilt, and for no better reason than God told us we could.[3]

We don't deserve the rest that He offers. But He offers it for us to enjoy as a free gift. Like other gifts of God, it needs to be received through faith.

REST WITHOUT GUILT

I love how Mark Buchanan defines what he calls "Sabbath's golden rule": "Cease from what is necessary [and] embrace that which gives life."[4] It's through this lens that we decide what should and shouldn't be part of our Sabbath time. What restores you and gives you life?

For me, as someone whose work often involves looking at a screen, it's to get outside and "work" in the garden. It's the least work-like thing I can think of. It gives life and restores my soul. However, if I were a professional landscaper, my Sabbath would most likely be entirely different.

If cooking a big dinner feels like work, then it gets nixed. Instead, I might opt for pancakes for dinner and ask my kids to help. Or if baking blueberry muffins is a life-giving activity (how could it not be?), then I will enjoy it on my Sabbath day.

Your Kick-Start

Want to jump ahead and complete your related challenge? Go to page 253 for details.

Regardless of how I choose to spend my time on this special day, my mind is oriented with gratitude toward Jesus—the Lord of the Sabbath.[5] I focus on His presence and allow Him to fill every moment of my day. Whether I'm chasing the kids around the yard, studying the book of Philippians, having dinner with friends, or praying as I hike through the forest, Jesus is on my mind and heart.

Without Him, there is no rest to be enjoyed. He is the source of everything that replenishes us and infuses our lives with joy. No matter how many balls we're juggling, with Jesus at our side, we can fully enjoy the rest that God has made available to each one of us.

CHAPTER 31

ENJOY IT ALL

My two-year-old daughter climbed into my lap the other night. She laid her head on my chest as we watched one of her favorite movies. As I held her in my arms, I began to get emotional. This might be the last time my daughter wants to sit on my lap to watch a movie. Tomorrow she might decide to proclaim her independence and sit next to me instead.

I keep having these moments with my kids. What if this is the last time they say that phrase, ask me to read them a bedtime story, or take my hand as we walk? The list is long. I realize they are growing up and these precious moments might soon be gone.

I don't know when it will happen, but I do know that I want to seize every opportunity that God has given me with my children and make the most of those moments. I can so clearly see a few years down the road when the kids are gone and I longingly look back for just one more hug from my little girl.

Even with that awareness, I'm constantly distracted by the nonstop busyness of parenting little kids. The frequent interruptions every time I'm chatting with Linda, the challenges of disciplining, and the difficulty of eking out just a few minutes of alone time with God. In the busyness and mundane, it's easy to forget to cherish the moments and end up letting the opportunity to create memories pass us by. It's a challenging season that I think in some ways represents life on earth.

Life is not for the faint of heart. It's full of obstacles, challenges, and mountains to be moved. And the world spins at a dizzying speed. But in the midst of it all, God has dispensed so much beauty. So much to enjoy.

I want to enjoy every moment—the mountain moments when I'm successful and the valley moments when I struggle. I want to take hold of the incredibly rich life available to me when I save all I can for His glory, earn all I can by working heartily for Him, give all I can with boldness, and enjoy Him in it all. God offers me the chance to serve Him well and to glorify Him, in each of these ways. And I want to embrace those moments before they are gone forever.

We're only going to be here for a short while—and then on to heaven. And as great as heaven will be, I'm convinced there will always be something special about our time spent on earth. When we had the opportunity to trust God without seeing Him. The opportunity to give without fully understanding what the eternal impact would be. The opportunity to walk by faith in a way that angels will never be able to understand.

In this lifetime, we get one shot to make the most of these opportunities. So I'll ask you a question poet Mary Oliver inspired me with years ago:

Tell me, what is it you plan to do
with your one wild and precious life?[1]

THE KICK-START

PART 4

16. ENJOY THE RIDE

(Read pages 227–32 for a refresher.)

For me, one of the most helpful keys to staying motivated has been understanding that progress isn't linear. You probably won't make the same amount of progress each day. Some days you may take significant steps forward, while other days you may seem to go backward. And the hardest work is required in the vision phase, where you aren't likely to see results as quickly.

Your challenge is to view your big financial goal through this lens. Whether you're wanting to save a down payment for a house, pay off your student loans, or buy your next car with cash, remember that your progress is likely to follow the curve laid out in the graph on page 231. So get comfortable with this, and brace yourself for the slow start. Soon you'll transition to the momentum phase, where things begin to move much faster.

○   Meditate on Galatians 6:9, and let God speak to you through this verse.

○   Write down a big financial goal you're working toward:

_____

○ Write down how you're going to celebrate when you reach the goal:

_____

_____

_____

○ Write down what you're going to do the next time you hit a bump in the road:

_____

_____

_____

17. EVALUATE YOUR DISCONTENT

(Read pages 239–41 for a refresher.)

In chapter 29, we talked about how easily discontentment can hinder joy, but we can fight back by changing our vantage point.

○ Spend 15 minutes prayerfully evaluating any areas of discontent in your life. If you're feeling stuck, try answering these questions:

- How do you feel about your house, car, clothing, job, and relationships?

- What possession do you yearn for and feel as if you can't be happy without?

- In what areas of your life are you feeling unsatisfied?

18. TELL YOURSELF—MAKE A LIST

(Read pages 242–43 for a refresher.)

A grateful heart yields tons of benefits like a stronger immune system, lower blood pressure, better sleep, and more energy, to name just a few.[1] Now let's really put that gratitude muscle to work and watch the benefits roll in!

○   Make a list of 50 things you're grateful for. They can be big or small. Keep going until you hit 50.

19. TELL THE WORLD

(Read pages 242–43 for a refresher.)

Thinking and writing about what we're grateful for helps us better appreciate what we've been given. In addition, sharing about it—especially when we give God the glory for it—can have a multiplying effect as it causes others to be grateful for the blessings in their lives.

○   Tell what you're grateful for.

Post on social media about something you're grateful for. Maybe it's a person in your life, something God has recently done in your heart, a recent financial breakthrough, or even your favorite pair of joggers. You get to choose. Oh, and be sure to tag us @seedtime so we can celebrate with you!

If you don't use social media, (1) you're my hero and (2) just go share with a friend in real life.

20. TAKE A SABBATH DAY

(Read pages 244–47 for a refresher.)

This challenge is to take a Sabbath day. As in no work, no email, no to-do list. Spend the day just enjoying the blessings that God has given you. First and foremost Himself. But also family and friends. Maybe a good devotional, a hike, a picnic, or a sunset. You might just find, like us, that this becomes a part of your weekly rhythm.

○   Schedule your Sabbath day and add it to your calendar.

○   Plan your Sabbath day to include things that help you rest and restore your soul.

THE FINAL STEP TO A RICH LIFE:
THE 1% CHALLENGE

The formula we've led you through in this book is to save, earn, and give all you can—while enjoying it all. That is the 40,000-foot view. Now I want to leave you with one simple, practical thing to do to make the most of the money God has entrusted to you. I call it the 1% challenge.

INCREASE YOUR SAVINGS AND GIVING BY 1% EVERY YEAR

One percent is so small you'd be surprised at the minimal impact it has on your budget. Yet each year your AUM and Net Given will grow, allowing you to manage God's money well on earth and store up treasure in heaven.

Most people find that they don't even notice an increase of 1% or 2%, but even if you are convinced that you will, if you follow the four-part framework mentioned in chapter 13, you should be able to see your earnings increase by well over 2% each year.

And if you want to or feel called to do more or to increase that percentage more frequently, by all means go for it. But strive to make a 1% annual increase the bare minimum.

LET'S TAKE ACTION NOW

○ Set an annual reminder to increase what you save and give by 1%.

Do this step right now. Ask Siri, Alexa, Google, or any other robot of your choosing to remind you every year to do this. Or add it to your calendar—whether that be an e-calendar, your planner, or a puppies-and-kittens wall calendar. Use the tool that works best for you. But just do it.

You can schedule it one year from today or on the first of the year. We increase our savings and giving on my birthday each year. It's an opportunity to celebrate God's faithfulness in providing for us well enough to be able to increase by another 1%.

A SIMPLE START

If you're not sure what percentage to start with, then I would suggest starting with whatever you do right now. Do you already save 5% and give 5% a year? Bump that up to 6%. Maybe you give 10% and save 3%. Increase each number by 1%. If you're new to percentage giving and saving, then start with just 1% this first year.

> LINDA: Or best of all, pray and see how the Lord directs you. His leading might very well be out of your comfort zone, which is a good thing. Always obey those promptings. That's where the adventure lies! Good things are always on the other side of obedience.

DO IT NOW

Seriously, in case you ignored me before, grab your phone right now and add a yearly reminder to increase the amount you give and save by 1%.

When that time comes, you can pull out this book, review your highlights if you need a refresher, then adjust each amount by 1%. If you have automated your savings and giving (see chapter 5), then increase those automatic withdrawals by 1% across the board, whether it's to savings, to your 401(k), or to your giving recipients.

This will probably take you 5 to 10 minutes. One time each year.

Can you spare 5 to 10 minutes a year to improve your financial life now and increase your eternal impact?

TRUST THE PROCESS

I know this sounds too simple. The fact is that succeeding with money really is simple. It isn't always easy, but if you consistently take the steps, you will succeed. It won't happen overnight (though most people are surprised how fast things change). Trust the process and keep going.

Let me be your friend and coach nudging you to do this. You won't regret it. If you do nothing else but apply this one idea, I believe your mind will be blown (Ephesians 3:20 style)* when you look back 10 or 20 years from now at what God has done in your financial life.

ONE LAST THING

Imagine being a few years down the road with no money worries but complete confidence in God as your provider. Free from the shackles of debt and, instead of paying interest, earning interest. Loving your work and thriving in your business or career. Having the opportunity to give from the overflow in your life and loving every minute of it.

And then imagine taking your first steps in heaven and being ab-

---

* "He will achieve infinitely more than your greatest request, your most unbelievable dream, and exceed your wildest imagination!" (TPT).

solutely floored by the incredible impact of some simple decisions you made with your money.

You see, I believe money management is an act of worship.

Every day, you and I make decisions about how to spend our money. We have the opportunity to use it for God's glory, resulting in eternal impact. The Enemy knows this, and I believe that's part of why so much of the church has been in financial bondage.

He is actively working to destroy our financial lives. This may look like fear, guilt, and shame related to money, stirring up strife with our spouses, and keeping us broke so we can't take care of our families and have nothing to give. It's his goal to keep us on a hamster wheel—always running yet never making any progress. And if we're all just struggling to keep our heads above water, how are we going to help those around us?

It's time we flip the script. It's time for the church to rise up, quit following the world's flawed approach to money, and show the world a better way.

I believe we should be the ones with the resources to solve the world's difficult problems.

I believe we should be the ones that the world comes running to for financial advice.

I believe God can and should be glorified by how we handle our money.

Following the simple formula in this book has yielded an incredibly rich life for us. As you apply what you've read, I pray that it will for you as well.

THANK YOU FOR READING!

I t has been an honor sharing our work with you. If this book has added value to your life, would you consider one of the following?

- **Take a selfie with this book; post it, tag us (@seedtime), and hashtag the heck out of it.** And while you're at it share one thing you enjoyed about the book, and we might just share your brilliant insights with our community.

- **Leave an honest review where you bought it.** Reviews have a huge effect on a book's reach. We will need all the help we can get if we want this message to rise above the noise of the world's money books. Your honest review can make a huge impact.

- **Share it with friends or pastors.** Tell them about it, and let them borrow your copy, or if you think they won't return it,* you could just buy them a copy with the funds in your newly created Seed Account!

DON'T BE A STRANGER!

Linda and I always love connecting with like-minded people like you, so if you have any questions or just want to say hi, send us a DM @seedtime on Instagram.

---

* We all have friends like that, right?

We look forward to hearing from you and exploring how we can continue to add as much value to your life as possible!

In Him,
Bob and Linda Lotich

BONUS RESOURCES

Throughout this book I've included links to a bunch of free tools and resources to help you win with money. You can find all of them (and more) listed on this page for your convenience.

Oh, and just as an FYI, some of these are products that we sell, but as a thank-you for reading the book, you get them for free. If you want to get them for free, be sure to use the links listed below:

- AUM Worksheet: seedtime.com/aum

- Budgeting Template: seedtime.com/budgeting

- Credit Card Recommendations: seedtime.com/cc

- Debt Snowball Worksheet: seedtime.com/snowball

- Email Newsletter: seedtime.com/newsletter

- Fear-Setting Exercise Worksheet: seedtime.com /fearsetting

- Hello from Us: seedtime.com/hello

- Net Given Template: seedtime.com/ng

- "Remember Your Why" PDF: seedtime.com/why

- Roth IRA Tutorial: seedtime.com/roth

- Spending Tracker Recommendations: seedtime.com /cashflow

WHAT SHOULD YOU READ NEXT?

If you enjoyed the book, then you'll probably enjoy our free email newsletter. It's where we share our latest podcasts, articles, videos, money tips, encouragement, and tools and resources to help you win with money and use it to honor God.

You can sign up at seedtime.com/newsletter.

ACKNOWLEDGMENTS

These are just some of the amazing people who helped make this book possible. Each one had a significant impact on the creation of what you just read. If you happen to know or meet any of them, give them a high five—they deserve it.*

- Our parents
- Barb Albert
- Chad Allen
- Jessy Rei Argota
- Joshua Becker
- Chuck Bentley
- Tom and Stephanie Bills
- Jacob and Callie Blount
- Eric Brinker
- Jeff and Lauren Cantoni
- Scott and Michelle Cash
- James Clear

- Stephen Cook
- Max and Hannah Corwin
- Cory Edwards
- Chris Ferebee
- Pam Gibbs
- Jeff Goins
- Justin and Laura Gordey
- Shelly Griffin
- Bryan and Stacy Harris
- Risi Hatmaker

* So many amazing people helped with the project, and I'm sure I forgot some, so if your name should be on this list, I'm sorry. Let me know, and I'll put it in twice in the next book.

- Tammy Hatmaker
- Tori Hein
- Mary Hunt
- Millie Katina
- Kristel Kazda
- Dawn Kropp
- Bryan Lark
- Kenny MacKay
- Derrick Minyard
- Kathy Mitchell
- Phillip and Joanna Parkinson
- Peggy Pedroza

- Jordan Raynor
- Carrie Rocha
- Alex Seeley
- Adam Simon
- Ruth Soukup
- Andrew Stoddard
- Robby Valderrama
- Bryce Vernon
- Kim Von Fange
- Carlos Whittaker
- You! Yep, go on and high-five yourself!

Seriously, thanks again for picking up this book and reading. Linda and I are praying that as you apply what you've read and take the natural steps, God would unleash the supernatural so that you can walk in true financial freedom.

NOTES

Grateful acknowledgment is made to the following for permission to reprint previously published excerpts from their blog posts:

Bryan Harris: "11-Star Experience," originally published on video fruit.com on July 31, 2020. Used by permission of Bryan Harris. All rights reserved.

Mike Michalowicz: "Money Amplifies Your Character," originally published on mikemichalowicz.com on March 19, 2013. Used by permission of Mike Michalowicz. All rights reserved.

INTRODUCTION

1. John Wesley, "Sermon LXXXVII: The Danger of Riches," in *Sermons on Several Occasions* (London: Wesleyan Conference Office, 1864), 3:8.

CHAPTER 1: THE BATTLE IS HIS, BUT YOU HAVE TO SHOW UP

1. 2 Chronicles 20:12.

2. 2 Chronicles 20:15–17.

3. 1 Kings 18:46, NLT.

CHAPTER 3: THE NEVER 100 RULE

1. "5 Richest Boxing Matches," CBS Los Angeles, February 20, 2015, https://losangeles.cbslocal.com/2015/02/20/top-5-richest-boxing -matches.

2. "The Highest-Paid Athletes of All-Time," *Forbes,* December 6, 2016, www.forbes.com/pictures/mli45fgmmj/11-mike-tyson.

3. "2020–21 NBA Player Contracts," Basketball Reference, www .basketball-reference.com/contracts/players.html.

4. Kerri Anne Renzulli and Courtney Connley, "Here's What the Average NFL Player Makes in a Season," CNBC, February 1, 2019, www .cnbc.com/2019/02/01/heres-what-the-average-nfl-players-makes -in-a-season.html.

5. Chris Dudley, "Money Lessons Learned from Pro Athletes' Financial Fouls," CNBC, May 14, 2018, www.cnbc.com/2018/05/14 /money-lessons-learned-from-pro-athletes-financial-fouls.html.

6. Kanye West, "Gold Digger," featuring Jamie Foxx, *Late Registration,* 2005.

7. "How Income Volatility Interacts with American Families' Financial Security," Pew Charitable Trusts, March 9, 2017, www.pewtrusts .org/en/research-and-analysis/issue-briefs/2017/03/how-income -volatility-interacts-with-american-families-financial-security.

8. Kathleen Elkins, "A Janitor Secretly Amassed an $8 Million Fortune and Left Most of It to His Library and Hospital," CNBC, August 29, 2016, www.cnbc.com/2016/08/29/janitor-secretly-amassed-an -8-million-fortune.html.

CHAPTER 4: ATTENTION: WHEN PERFORMANCE IS MEASURED, IT IMPROVES

1. "The History of Money," PBS, October 26, 1996, www.pbs.org/wgbh /nova/article/history-money.

2. Proverbs 27:23, NASB.

3. John 16:33.

4. Sherri Johnson, "Applying Pearson's Law to Recruiting and Retention," RISMedia, https://rismedia.com/2020/07/22/applying -pearsons-law-recruiting-retention.

5. Chris McChesney, Sean Covey, and Jim Huling, *The 4 Disciplines of Execution: Achieving Your Wildly Important Goals,* rev. ed. (New York: Simon & Schuster, 2021), 77.

CHAPTER 5: AUTOMATE: NEVER DEPEND ON WILLPOWER

1. Bruce Bartlett, "Tax Withholding Still Controversial After 70 Years," *Economix* (blog), *New York Times,* October 22, 2013, https:// economix.blogs.nytimes.com/2013/10/22/tax-withholding-still -controversial-after-70-years.

2. James Clear, *Atomic Habits: Tiny Changes, Remarkable Results* (New York: Avery, 2018), 24, 27.

CHAPTER 6: ADJUST: IF YOU FIND YOURSELF IN A HOLE, STOP DIGGING

1. Philippians 4:19.

2. Ephesians 3:20, NKJV.

CHAPTER 8: HOW TO SPEND MORE ON WHAT YOU LOVE

1. Ramit Sethi, "Money Dials: Why You Spend the Way You Do," I Will Teach You to Be Rich, December 21, 2018, www.iwillteachyoutoberich .com/blog/money-dials.

2. James Clear, *Atomic Habits: Tiny Changes, Remarkable Results* (New York: Avery, 2018), 82.

CHAPTER 9: HOW TO SPEND SMARTER (AND THE BUBBLE TAURUS)

1. Doug DeMuro, "At What Mileage Should You 'Stay Away' from a Car?," Autotrader, January 13, 2017, www.autotrader.com/car-news /what-mileage-should-you-stay-away-car-260881.

2. Josh Clark, "Are Modern Cars Less Problematic?," HowStuffWorks, https://auto.howstuffworks.com/under-the-hood/diagnosing-car -problems/mechanical/cars-less-problematic.htm.

3. "2020 Ford Fusion Cost to Own," Edmunds, www.edmunds.com /ford/fusion/2020/cost-to-own/#style=401799037; "2020 Honda Civic Cost to Own," Edmunds, www.edmunds.com/honda/civic /2020/cost-to-own/#style=401823139.

4. Zechariah 4:10, NLT.

CHAPTER 10: THE HIDDEN EXPERIMENT WE'RE ALL PART OF

1. Jason Steele, "The History of Credit Cards," Creditcards.com, May 24, 2021, www.creditcards.com/credit-card-news/history-of-credit-cards.

2. "US Consumer Debt," Wikimedia, https://upload.wikimedia.org/wikipedia/commons/4/43/US_consumer_debt.png.

3. *The Complex Story of American Debt: Liabilities in Family Balance Sheets* (Philadelphia: Pew Charitable Trusts, July 2015), 15, www.pewtrusts.org/~/media/assets/2015/07/reach-of-debt-report_artfinal.pdf?la=en.

4. Craig Hill, *Five Wealth Secrets 96% of Us Don't Know* (Littleton, CO: Family Foundations International, 2012), 54.

5. David Gal and Blakeley B. McShane, "To Beat Debt, Consider Starting Small," Kellogg Insight, January 8, 2014, https://insight.kellogg.northwestern.edu/article/to_beat_debt_consider_starting_small; Alexander L. Brown and Joanna N. Lahey, "Small Victories: Creating Intrinsic Motivation in Task Completion and Debt Repayment," Consumer Financial Protection Bureau Research Panel 2, May 7, 2015, slide 19, https://files.consumerfinance.gov/f/documents/P2d_-_Brown_-_Small_Victories.pdf.

THE KICK-START: PART 1

1. Friedrich Nietzsche, quoted in Viktor E. Frankl, *Man's Search for Meaning: An Introduction to Logotherapy*, 4th ed., trans. Ilse Lasch (Boston: Beacon, 1992), 109.

PART 2: EARN ALL YOU CAN

1. Ephesians 3:20.

2. Colossians 3:23, ESV.

CHAPTER 12: MONEY IS A TERRIBLE MASTER BUT A GREAT SERVANT

1. Erin Blakemore, "This Mine Fire Has Been Burning for Over 50 Years," History.com, April 26, 2019, www.history.com/news/mine-fire-burning-more-50-years-ghost-town.

2.   "The National Burn Rate Is Going Up—Literally," Face the Facts USA, August 26, 2013, https://facethefactsusa.org/facts/the-national -burn-rate-is-going-up--literally.

3.   Proverbs 27:20, KJV.

4.   New World Encyclopedia, s.v. "John D. Rockefeller," www .newworldencyclopedia.org/entry/John_D._Rockefeller.

5.   Jonathan Swift, quoted in Thomas Roscoe, "Life and Works of Jonathan Swift," in *The Works of Jonathan Swift* (London: Henry Washbourne, 1841), 1:lxxxii.

6.   John Piper, *Future Grace: The Purifying Power of the Promises of God,* rev. ed. (Colorado Springs: Multnomah Books, 2012), 324.

7.   Matthew 19:16–22.

8.   Luke 19:1–10.

9.   Craig Hill, *Five Wealth Secrets 96% of Us Don't Know* (Littleton, CO: Family Foundations International, 2012), 40.

10.   Mike Michalowicz, "Money Amplifies Your Character," Mike Michalowicz, March 19, 2013, https://mikemichalowicz.com/money -amplifies-your-character.

11.   Psalm 51:10; 139:23–24.

12.   Philippians 4:19.

13.   Philippians 4:11.

14.   2 Corinthians 9:8; James 1:5.

CHAPTER 13: FOUR KEYS TO EARNING MORE IN THE DIGITAL ERA

1.   Scott Adams, "Career Advice," Dilbert.Blog, July 20, 2007, https:// dilbertblog.typepad.com/the_dilbert_blog/2007/07/career-advice .html.

CHAPTER 14: CALLING AND PASSION: FISH DON'T CLIMB TREES

1.   Psalm 139:14; Ephesians 2:10, NLT.

2.   "Everybody Is a Genius," Quote Investigator, April 6, 2013, https:// quoteinvestigator.com/2013/04/06/fish-climb.

3. Steve Jobs, "2005 Stanford Commencement Address" (speech, Stanford University, Stanford, CA, June 12, 2005), https://news .stanford.edu/2005/06/14/jobs-061505.

4. *Chariots of Fire,* directed by Hugh Hudson, Enigma Productions, 1981.

5. Jeff Goins, *The Art of Work: A Proven Path to Discovering What You Were Meant to Do* (Nashville: Nelson Books, 2015), 20.

6. Goins, *Art of Work,* 122.

7. Colossians 3:23, ESV.

8. Romans 8:28.

9. John 6:5–13.

10. James 2:17–20.

11. Goins, *Art of Work,* 35.

CHAPTER 15: EDUCATION: KEEP LEARNING AND HONING YOUR CRAFT

1. Ali Montag and Tom Huddleston Jr., "How Gamer Tyler 'Ninja' Blevins Went from Working at a Fast Food Joint to Making Almost $1 Million a Month Playing Fortnite," CNBC, January 4, 2019, www .cnbc.com/2019/01/04/ninja-blevins-from-a-fast-food-job-to -millionaire-fortnite-gamer.html.

2. Malcolm Gladwell, *Outliers: The Story of Success* (New York: Little, Brown, 2008), 39–40.

3. Proverbs 22:29, TPT.

CHAPTER 16: SOLVE A PROBLEM OR MAKE SOMETHING BETTER

1. Britannica Kids, s.v. "Johannes Gutenberg," https://kids.britannica .com/students/article/Johannes-Gutenberg/274706.

2. Dave Roos, "7 Ways the Printing Press Changed the World," History.com, August 28, 2019, www.history.com/news/printing-press -renaissance.

3. Isaac Newton, letter to Robert Hooke, 1675, Historical Society of Pennsylvania, https://discover.hsp.org/Record/dc-9792/Description #tabnav.

4. Tony Robbins, *Money: Master the Game* (New York: Simon & Schuster, 2016), 6.

5. Brian Chesky, quoted in Reid Hoffman, "How to Scale a Magical Experience: 4 Lessons from Airbnb's Brian Chesky," Reid Hoffman, May 22, 2018, https://reid.medium.com/how-to-scale -a-magical-experience-4-lessons-from-airbnbs-brian-chesky -eca0a182f3e3.

6. Bryan Harris, "11-Star Experience," Growth Tools, July 31, 2020, https://videofruit.com/blog/11-star-experience.

7. Chesky, quoted in Hoffman, "How to Scale."

8. Psalm 75:6–7.

CHAPTER 17: DEMAND: GIVE THEM WHAT THEY WANT

1. "The Story of Levi Strauss," Levi Strauss & Co., March 14, 2013, www.levistrauss.com/2013/03/14/the-story-of-levi-strauss; *Encyclopaedia Britannica,* s.v. "Levi Strauss & Co.," www.britannica.com /topic/Levi-Strauss-and-Co.

CHAPTER 18: QUIT LIVING AS IF THE PURPOSE OF LIFE IS TO ARRIVE SAFELY AT DEATH

The chapter title is taken from Mark Batterson, *Chase the Lion: If Your Dream Doesn't Scare You, It's Too Small* (Colorado Springs: Multnomah, 2016), 3.

1. Matthew 14:22–33.

2. John 10:10.

3. Batterson, *Chase the Lion,* 3.

4. Batterson, *Chase the Lion,* 2.

5. Tim Ferriss, "Fear-Setting: The Most Valuable Exercise I Do Every Month," *Tim Ferriss* (blog), May 15, 2017, https://tim.blog/2017/05 /15/fear-setting. The fear-setting exercise described in this chapter is adapted from Ferriss's exercise.

6. Ferriss, "Fear-Setting."

7. Ferriss, "Fear-Setting."

8. Ferriss, "Fear-Setting."

PART 3: GIVE ALL YOU CAN

1.   Luke 12:33, TPT.

2.   Warren Buffett, quoted in Mary Buffett and David Clark, *The Tao of Warren Buffett: Warren Buffett's Words of Wisdom* (New York: Scribner, 2006), 145.

3.   Randy Alcorn, *The Treasure Principle: Unlocking the Secret of Joyful Giving*, rev. ed. (Colorado Springs: Multnomah, 2017), 48.

4.   Luke 12:33, TPT.

CHAPTER 19: EVERYTHING I THOUGHT ABOUT GIVING WAS WRONG

1.   Acts 20:35.

2.   2 Corinthians 9:7, NLT.

3.   2 Corinthians 9:10, AMP.

4.   Acts 20:35.

5.   Christian Smith and Hilary Davidson, *The Paradox of Generosity: Giving We Receive, Grasping We Lose* (New York: Oxford University Press, 2014), book description.

CHAPTER 20: WHY WE BEGAN "GIVING OUR AGE"

1.   Romans 8:28, NLT.

2.   2 Corinthians 9:7.

CHAPTER 21: GIVING IS LIKE GARDENING

1.   1 Kings 17:12.

2.   1 Kings 17:15–16.

3.   Genesis 8:22.

4.   2 Corinthians 9:6.

5.   2 Corinthians 9:10–11, NLT.

6.   Matthew 4:6.

7.   Matthew 4:7.

8.   2 Corinthians 9:10, TPT.

9.   Charles F. Stanley, "The Principle of Sowing and Reaping," In Touch Ministries, July 6, 2014, www.intouch.org/read/life-principle-6-the -principle-of-sowing-and-reaping.

10. R. G. LeTourneau, quoted in James A. Scudder Jr., "God Has a Bigger Shovel," InGrace, https://ingrace.us/february-9th-10th-god-has -a-bigger-shovel.

11. Francis Chan, "From Pastor to Millionaire . . . Giver!," Generous Giving, https://generousgiving.org/francis-chan-from-pastor-to -millionaire-giver.

12. Chan, "From Pastor to Millionaire . . . Giver!"

CHAPTER 22: THE DANCING GORILLA

1.   Trafton Drew, Melissa L.-H. Võ, and Jeremy M. Wolfe, "The Invisible Gorilla Strikes Again: Sustained Inattentional Blindness in Expert Observers," *Psychological Science* 24, no. 9 (2013): 1848–53, www.ncbi.nlm.nih.gov/pmc/articles/PMC3964612.

2.   Ann Pietrangelo, "What the Baader-Meinhof Phenomenon Is and Why You May See It Again . . . and Again," Healthline, December 17, 2019, www.healthline.com/health/baader-meinhof -phenomenon.

3.   Luke 5:4–8.

4.   Acts 20:35.

CHAPTER 23: SECRETS OF SIX-FIGURE GIVERS

1.   Ephesians 3:20, TLB.

2.   Zechariah 4:10, NLT.

3.   Matthew 6:33, CEV.

4.   Genesis 17:17; 18:12.

5.   Genesis 37:5–11.

6.   Luke 1:30–35.

7.   Mark Batterson, quoted in Kevin Kruse, "Dare to Dream Big: Your Goals Should Feel Scary," LinkedIn, June 17, 2017, www.linkedin .com/pulse/dare-dream-big-your-goals-should-feel-scary-kevin -kruse.

CHAPTER 24: NET GIVEN: THE MOST IMPORTANT METRIC

1. Sherri Johnson, "Applying Pearson's Law to Recruiting and Retention," RISMedia, https://rismedia.com/2020/07/22/applying-pearsons-law-recruiting-retention.

2. Camilla Eyring Kimball, quoted in Amanda Kae Fronk, "Ministering with Kindness," BYU Speeches, January 20, 2016, https://speeches.byu.edu/posts/ministering-with-kindness.

3. John 10:10.

4. Matthew 6:33.

CHAPTER 25: FOUR TIPS TO MAKE GIVING EASIER AND MORE FUN

1. Andy Stanley (@AndyStanley), Twitter, December 29, 2015, 12:07 p.m., https://twitter.com/andystanley/status/681914412920258560.

2. John D. Rockefeller, quoted in Andrew McNair, "Why I Tithe—and So Should You," *Forbes*, April 21, 2014, www.forbes.com/sites/learnvest/2014/04/21/why-i-tithe-and-so-should-you.

3. 2 Corinthians 9:7.

4. Matthew 25:21.

5. Tim Mohns, "A Perfectly Good Crisis," Generous Giving, https://generousgiving.org/media/videos/tim-mohns-a-perfectly-good-crisis.

CHAPTER 26: THE BUTTERFLY EFFECT

1. *Encyclopaedia Britannica*, s.v. "Edward Lorenz," www.britannica.com/biography/Edward-Lorenz.

2. Andy Andrews, "The Butterfly Effect by Andy Andrews," YouTube video, 9:45, June 19, 2013, www.youtube.com/watch?v=mo6fBAT8f-s.

3. "List of Products Made from the Peanut by Dr. George Washington Carver," Tuskegee University, www.tuskegee.edu/support-tu/george-washington-carver/carver-peanut-products; "List of Products Made from Sweet Potato by George Washington Carver," Tuskegee University, www.tuskegee.edu/support-tu/george-washington-carver/carver-sweet-potato-products.

4. Billy Graham, *Facing Death and the Life After* (Waco, TX: Word Books, 1987), 267.

PART 4: ENJOY IT ALL

1. John 10:10, ESV.
2. 1 Timothy 6:17.
3. C. S. Lewis, *Mere Christianity* (New York: HarperOne, 2001), 49.

CHAPTER 27: ENJOY WHAT PROGRESS ACTUALLY LOOKS LIKE

1. John Soforic, *The Wealthy Gardener: Life Lessons on Prosperity Between Father and Son* (Mount Pleasant, PA: self-pub., 2018), 355.
2. James Clear, *Atomic Habits: Tiny Changes, Remarkable Results* (New York: Avery, 2018), 20.
3. Jacob A. Riis, *The Making of an American* (New York: Grosset & Dunlap, 1901), 253.
4. Galatians 6:9.

CHAPTER 28: ENJOY SPENDING

1. Kiona N. Smith, "Everything We Know About the Isolated Sentinelese People of North Sentinel Island," *Forbes,* November 30, 2018, www.forbes.com/sites/kionasmith/2018/11/30/everything-we -know-about-the-isolated-sentinelese-people-of-north-sentinel -island.
2. Matthew 7:3–5, ESV.
3. Matthew 26:14–15; John 12:1–6.
4. Arthur Leger, "God Likes Gold—The Uses and Value of Gold in the Bible," LinkedIn, January 17, 2017, www.linkedin.com/pulse/god -likes-gold-uses-value-bible-arthur-leger.
5. 1 Timothy 6:17.

CHAPTER 29: ENJOY WHAT YOU HAVE

1. Ron Chernow, *Titan: The Life of John D. Rockefeller, Sr.,* 2nd ed. (New York: Vintage Books, 2004), 556.
2. Proverbs 27:20, KJV.

3. Robert A. Emmons, *Thanks! How Practicing Gratitude Can Make You Happier* (Boston: Houghton Mifflin, 2008), book description.

4. Heather Craig, "The Research on Gratitude and Its Link with Love and Happiness," Positivepsychology.com, February 27, 2021, https://positivepsychology.com/gratitude-research.

5. Robert Emmons, "Why Gratitude Is Good," Greater Good, November 16, 2010, https://greatergood.berkeley.edu/article/item/why _gratitude_is_good.

CHAPTER 30: ENJOY REST

1. Joshua 1:13, NASB.

2. Matthew McCreary, "Chick-fil-A Makes More per Restaurant Than McDonald's, Starbucks and Subway Combined . . . and It's Closed on Sundays," *Entrepreneur*, September 25, 2018, www.entrepreneur .com/article/320615.

3. Mark Buchanan, *The Rest of God: Restoring Your Soul by Restoring Sabbath* (Nashville: Thomas Nelson, 2006), 93.

4. Buchanan, *Rest of God*, 129.

5. Matthew 12:8.

CHAPTER 31: ENJOY IT ALL

1. Mary Oliver, "The Summer Day," Library of Congress, www.loc.gov /programs/poetry-and-literature/poet-laureate/poet-laureate -projects/poetry-180/all-poems/item/poetry-180-133/the-summer -day.

THE KICK-START: PART 4

1. Robert Emmons, "Why Gratitude Is Good," Greater Good, November 16, 2010, https://greatergood.berkeley.edu/article/item/why _gratitude_is_good.

ABOUT THE AUTHOR

Bob Lotich, CEPF®, is a high-performance financial coach and has been named a top-twenty influencer in personal finance. His award-winning website, seedtime.com, and *SeedTime Money* podcast have reached over 50 million people in the past decade.

He loves sharing the results of his money experiments, from budgeting hacks and investing strategies to radical giving and yearlong sabbaticals, along with other timeless financial instruction from the Bible. He and his wife, Linda, live in Franklin, Tennessee, with their three children.

Your Next Three Steps

1. Get our free *Simple Money* email newsletter.

Join over 100,000 others who get a regular dose of my best tips, inspiration, encouragement, and devotions to help you continue your journey to true financial freedom. Get it at seedtime.com/newsletter.

2. Get our free *SeedTime Money* podcast.

Join Linda and I as we share real-life case studies, encouragement, and our best secrets and tips to unlock your earning, saving, and giving potential. Start listening now at seedtime.com/smp.

3. Enroll in one of our courses.

Use our in-depth training courses to get extraordinary results even faster.

The Real Money Method

This reimagined approach to budgeting takes the One-Category Budget (from chapter 7) to the next level. It is so quick you can do it during a commercial break and so easy your spouse will be on board, and it works even if you've always struggled to stick with a budget. It is by far our most popular course, for good reason—it just works.

10x Investing

This course details my passive wealth-building strategy that requires only about an hour per year to maintain. This is a beginner to intermediate level course designed to help you invest your first $100 or as much as you want! You'll learn to invest wisely, reduce risk, and begin making your money work for you.

**Learn more about these and our other courses
at seedtime.com/courses**